Identity and Intimacy in Marriage:
A Study of Couples

Susan Krauss Whitbourne
Joyce B. Ebmeyer

Identity and Intimacy in Marriage

A Study of Couples

Springer-Verlag
New York Berlin Heidelberg
London Paris Tokyo Hong Kong

Susan Krauss Whitbourne
Department of Psychology
University of Massachusetts at Amherst
Amherst, MA 01003, U.S.A.

Joyce B. Ebmeyer
Monroe 1 Board of Cooperative Educational Services
Fairport, NY 14450, U.S.A.

Library of Congress Cataloging-in-Publication Data
Whitbourne, Susan Krauss.
    Identity and intimacy in marriage: a study of couples/Susan
Krauss Whitbourne, Joyce B. Ebmeyer.
        p.   cm.
    Includes bibliographical references.
    ISBN 0-387-97012-6 (alk. paper)
    1. Married people—United States—Psychology—Case studies.
    2. Identity (Psychology)—United States—Case studies.   3. Intimacy
(Psychology)—Case studies.   I. Ebmeyer, Joyce B.   II. Title.
    HQ728.W48   1990
    306.872—dc20   89-27583

Printed on acid-free paper.

Typeset by Best-Set Typographers, Hong Kong.
Printed and bound by Edwards Brothers Inc., Ann Arbor, Michigan.
Printed in the United States of America.

9 8 7 6 5 4 3 2 1

ISBN 0-387-97012-6 Springer-Verlag New York Berlin Heidelberg
ISBN 3-540-97012-6 Springer-Verlag Berlin Heidelberg New York

To our husbands

Preface

Through the research on which this book reports, we have been given the unique opportunity to explore the complex nature of two of the most important issues in the lives of adults: identity and intimacy. It is with deep gratitude that we give credit to the 80 individuals in our sample who allowed us to explore these processes in their lives.

Our purpose in writing this book was, in some ways, a modest one. Both of us believed that research on the Eriksonian concept of intimacy was deficient in that it was limited to the reports of individuals about themselves. We maintained that this kind of research could provide only a narrow, and probably biased, view of the intimacy development of individuals. By obtaining complementary responses to the intimacy interview from both partners in a marital relationship, we hope to pave a new path that future researchers in this area will follow. Beyond this methodological advance, we intended that this book's theoretical focus could put a new perspective on the well-trodden path of research on marriage. This more ambitious goal is one that we faced with some trepidation. The literature on marital adjustment and satisfaction is vast and potentially overwhelming. Is there a place or even a need, we wondered, for yet another approach to understanding the processes involved in close dyadic relationships? However, as our analyses of the data progressed, we felt increasingly confident that our perspective could have value. The identity of the individual as a spouse provides a unique framework for examining the intimacy of married couples.

There are many individuals in addition to our sample to whom we owe thanks for helping us complete this study. Gerry Gladstein and Shelly Malett of the University of Rochester were helpful in guiding the early formulations of the study. Priscilla Corwin, Kim Post, Jennifer Rusin, and Sande Sommers, graduate students at the University of Rochester, spent many hours rating the dyadic communication excerpts of the 40 couples. Karen Wampler willingly sent us the communications rating manual used as the basis for the one in our study. We are also grateful for the inspiration and insights offered by George Levinger at the University of Massachusetts at Amherst, whose thoughtful comments led us to develop the coding and analytic scheme that form the basis for this book. The assistance of Helen Knights and Steve Becker for their work in developing the coding system for the intimacy interview is also greatly valued.

Finally, we are grateful to the members of our families for their invaluable support and contributions to this book. To Julius Rock and Lisa Krauss Rock, for making their kitchen table available for our "holiday" conferences, to Stacey Whitbourne and Jennifer O'Brien for their patient acceptance of their mother's burying herself under piles of transcripts for yet another time, and to Richard O'Brien, for his unwavering support in the process, we owe our deepest thanks. We also will be forever thankful to Jim Ebmeyer for his typing of the many drafts of the original document on which the present volume is based. His moral support was vital to the completion of the research. Jeff, Chris, and Lynn Ebmeyer probably do not remember their mother when she was not involved in research or writing, and reminded her that "you can't quit now" when she was discouraged. Our thanks also go to Jan De Mocker and Jason Berman for their support and many helpful comments.

This book has represented an adventure for both of us through the vicissitudes, tribulations, and joys of the life of married couples. We hope our efforts to summarize what we found will be as stimulating and impressive to our readers as they have been to us.

Amherst, Massachusetts   Susan Krauss Whitbourne
Rochester, New York   Joyce B. Ebmeyer

Contents

1
Perspectives on Intimacy

The topic of intimacy holds a special fascination to most adults. Perhaps this is in part because close relationships penetrate into the depths of our own innermost beings. There is also an alluring intrigue, almost a voyeurism, in finding out the details of how other people cope with the pleasures and frustrations of remaining in intimate relationships. How, for instance, do other married people handle conflict? How do couples negotiate child care? If one is not married, questions such as these are just as pertinent, if not more so. It is no coincidence, given this high level of interest in the topic, that there are virtually thousands of books and magazine articles on intimacy and marital communication in the popular press and media.

The primary purpose of this book is to illustrate how intimate relationships in marriage are vital products of the identities of the two individuals who make up that relationship. It is true that the "relationship" has a quality and a life of its own, as the marriage manuals emphasize. However, a more compelling influence on the intimacy between husband and wife can be found, we believe, within the view of self-in-a-relationship that each partner separately holds. There is a dynamic process that occurs over time as this view changes due to development within the individual and developments in the couple. In our study of couples married for from 5 to 20 years, we hoped to provide insight into the kinds of adjustments that couples make over time in their identities within relationships.[1] We believe that the conclusions reached in our study can have important implications for researchers in the field of intimacy, as well as for clinicians whose work involves the treatment of marital and family difficulties.

A second function that we hope to fulfill is to clarify an essential feature of Erikson's (1963) theory, a widely used reference in works on adult intimacy. Most workers in the field of intimacy regard the individual's self-

---

[1] This is a cross-sectional study, so it will not be possible to make inferences about change over time. Comparisons of processes used by couples married differing lengths of time can only result in suggestions of developmental processes, the existence of which must be verified by longitudinal research.

report as an accurate description of his or her potential to enter into close, long-term relationships. As will soon become clear to the reader of this book, such a view is both unrealistic and inaccurate. Statements by individuals about their relationships taken out of context from what their partners say will reflect, simply, their identity as intimate partners rather than an indication of how intimate they can be.

Our third goal in writing this book is to show that any typology would be far too simplistic to capture the many complexities involved in the inter-actions between adults involved in long-term relationships. Some types will, no doubt, stand out in the descriptions of couples presented in this book. Hints of autonomous, companionate, merged, and conflict-habituated types will appear in the excerpts presented in the subsequent chapters. However, these are hints, not consistent themes. Elements of all types can be found in all marriages. What is also clear is that couples operate according to their model of what kind of relationship they have, and this model may or may not be a shared one. Again, the role of individual identities will turn out to be the crucial factor in determining the nature of the couple's interaction. The focus of this book will be, then, not on typologies, but on a microanalysis of processes through which people's identities influence and are influenced by their close relationships.

A Model of Identity in Relationships

The primary definition of adult identity on which our work is based is taken from Erikson's (1963) theory. According to Erikson, identity is a psy-chosocial construct, a product of factors unique to the individual combined with exposure to a social context. Erikson considered identity to be an important issue for adolescents, but also to be a life-long concern under-pinning later developmental tasks in adulthood. The attainment of intimacy is one of these tasks.

In earlier research by Whitbourne (1986b), adult identity was theorized to have as its content the individual's various self-conceptions: the physical self, the psychological self, and the social self. These conceptions are integrated into a consistent view of the self as enduring over time. The contents of identity, for most mentally healthy adults is of the self as "loving" to family members, "competent" at work, and "good" in an ethical sense. Interviews of adults concerning their identities revealed that they attempt to maintain this identity through a Piagetian-like process of assimilation. This "identity process" of assimilation is one of two basic forces that underlie the adult's interaction with the environment. The other identity process that complements assimilation is identity accommodation.

Identity assimilation is proposed to work in the following way. The adult's identity as a loving, competent, and good person serves to act as a filter through which experiences relevant to the self are perceived. Some of the methods used for the purpose of assimilation are similar to the defense mechanisms discussed by psychoanalytic theorists. The unique quality of assimilation as an identity process is that it has as its goal the preservation of the adult's particular view of the self, whatever that may be. Assimilation is the force that conserves and protects the adult's identity over time. It is the primary mechanism through which the adult maintains a sense of consistency and stability. There are experiences, however, that cannot be transformed by assimilation into perceptions that are consistent with the individual's current identity. When these occur, the identity process of accommodation is brought into play.

Identity accommodation is the process through which adults change their identities so that they are more congruent with experiences. Through accommodation, the adult makes changes in identity that correspond to the objective reality of life events. Perhaps one is fired from a job on the basis of incompetence. Accommodation would be the process responsible for recognizing that the fault lay not in the employer but in one's own limitations.

Both assimilation and accommodation are considered necessary, as in Piaget's theory, to the development of an identity that is adapted to the adult's environment. Ideally, the individual is able to maintain a dynamic equilibrium between the two processes, using whichever one is required according to the circumstances at the moment. At times, however, there may be a disequilibrium when one process prevails over the other. To maintain adaptation to the environment requires that the adult correct this imbalance and bring into play the underused identity process.

Because of its highly interactive nature, the identity an adult has as a partner in an intimate relationship (referred to here as "spouse identity") presents a special case in the study of adult identity. The interviews analyzed in this study revealed that there are three components to the spouse identity: views of the self as an intimate person, models of intimate relationships, and views of the partner in one's actual relationship.[2] The views of the self as an intimate person include one's perception of the self as able to share and express feelings of tenderness, able to resolve conflicts, and able to negotiate issues of control. Models of intimate relationships include ideas about egalitarianism, the value of sharing, and different styles of communicating and resolving conflict. Views of the partner as a spouse include the perceptions of the partner's potential for intimacy, other personality attributes, and ideas about what the partner thinks about oneself. Spouse identity is theorized to emerge from the individual's past life experiences of growing up in a family, of having earlier romantic relationships, and of being exposed to cultural ideals of love and marriage. Experiences within the marriage present a constant source of potential refinement of this identity through accommodation.

---

[2] For ease of presentation, the term "spouse" will be applied to the individual being discussed and the term "partner" to that individual's mate.

Marital interactions provide the individual with many opportunities to modify one's identity as an intimate person and one's model of an ideal relationship. These same interactions serve to define and redefine the perception of one's partner. Interactions with one's partner also can serve to modify one's identity in areas outside the relationship.

The way that identity processes operate in intimate relationships parallels closely the proposed model of individual identity processes. A woman, for example, marries with a certain identity of herself as an intimate person, a desired model of a relationship, and certain perceptions of her husband. Through identity assimilation, her experiences become transformed so that these three realms of her spouse identity are maintained intact. Through assimilation, she minimizes the implications of differences between her identity as a spouse and the various realms of her experiences within the marriage. However, if the assimilation process operates unchecked, the woman will find that a disequilibrium exists that threatens the stability of her relationship. Either she or her husband will have to use accommodation in order to restore balance. Through accommodation, she can revise her spouse identity so that it is more in keeping with the reality of the relationship. Conversely, or at the same time, she may accommodate more and more to her husband's personal qualities, so that their spouse identities become more closely aligned. Which type of accommodation is more adaptive to the relationship is a question that will be explored in depth in this study.

Forms of Identity Assimilation in Couples

Throughout our description of this study, we will be using direct quotes taken from the interviews of husbands and wives in which they were asked identical questions about their marriage. Analysis of these segments, along with numerical counts of categorical responses, forms the basis for the inferences we have drawn about the interaction between identity and intimacy in marriage. A similar process was used in the analysis of individual identity interviews in the study by Whitbourne (1986b). With couples, there was the additional advantage (and complication) of being able to compare the responses of both spouses.

In this section, we will provide the reader with examples of typical identity processes as inferred from the intimacy interviews. These examples form the core of our analyses presented throughout the book. As will become evident, there are many variations on these identity processes. The examples here serve to define and highlight the major features of these processes. We begin with examples of assimilation.

Denial and assertion. Theoretically, denial is one of the most straightforward modes of identity assimilation. Any dissonant information that would conflict with one's identity is magically erased when its existence is simply and rigidly ignored. To rate denial from the response of an individual, as in the identity interview, a considerable amount of inference is needed. Indeed, it is generally not possible to be certain that respondents are denying problems since if they were, there would be no indication of them in the interview. The term "defensive rigidity" is therefore used to describe this when, in the identity interview, a respondent appears to be minimizing a lack of correspondence between identity and experiences. With data from couples, it is possible to circumvent this problem and rate denial more directly. The husband is considered to be using denial if the wife, for instance, said there was a problem in some aspect of the relationship, and he said there was none. It is possible that the wife is creating problems where none exists, but the fact that a problem within the marriage is not alluded to by the husband suggests at least the potential that he is presenting an unduly optimistic portrayal of the relationship.

Another assimilative tactic related to denial is the flat assertion that the couple has a relationship that fits with the spouse's own identity when the partner presents evidence that certain elements of such a relationship are lacking. The typical form that this type of assimilation took was for one spouse, for example, the wife, to say that the couple discusses "everything" and for her husband to say that they discuss very little, or for her to say that they spend "all" their free time together and for him to say "hardly any." As with denial, it is possible that the wife is correct and the husband is being inordinately negative. The husband may be feeling neglected or ignored for some reason, and therefore distorting his experiences within the relationship to fit this unfavorable identity as a spouse. It is nevertheless clear that some kind of assimilative process of assertion is going on by at least one of the partners, though, since they cannot both be correct.

Justification of one's own or spouse's behavior. Self-justification is an assimilation mode used by individuals to allow their experiences to fit into their existing identities. As used by spouses regarding their identities in relationships, self-justification can become translated into "other"-justification. This took place in the responses of wives, but not husbands. The husband was excused for whatever limitations he possessed by attributing these to inherited personality traits, problems in the situation, or to flaws in the wife. Other-justification is a more complicated process than denial or assertion, and it may be said to involve at least some accommodation to the reality of an imperfect relationship. However, this accommodation is only a fleeting one, as it is quickly replaced by an unrealistic attempt to minimize the husband's weaknesses. For their part, husbands were more likely to use self-justification, in which they found ways to excuse or rationalize limitations in their own performance as spouses.

Idealization of spouse. To take other-justification to its more extreme form, a spouse might transform the partner's qualities into a paragon of virtue. The partner not only is excused for any weaknesses, but is seen as so perfect that the possibility of having any flaws is totally eliminated. A counterpart to this process might be self-derogation, where whatever problems are acknowledged are attributed to the self. Although this type of assimilation thereby reflects unfavorably upon one's own individual characteristics, it allows the person to maintain the identity of a spouse in a good relationship. Again, this was a process seen in wives but not husbands. Some possible reasons for this difference will be discussed in later chapters.

External projection of problems. External projection of problems is a strategy that individuals use to allow their identities as spouses to fit with potentially nonconfirmatory experiences in the relationship. It is a variant of identity projection, a mode of assimilation observed in individuals when describing their own identities. Identity projection, as an individual identity process, combines defensive rigidity (excluding problems from awareness) and self-justification (making excuses or trying to appear in the right). As applied to couples, this form of assimilation becomes a process of looking to problems outside the relationship to account for discrepancies between one's identity as a spouse and experiences within the relationship at the time. The interference of children, job obligations, in-laws, and community responsibilities all may be recruited for the purpose of protecting one's identity as a spouse from the realization that the relationship is fundamentally flawed.

Forms of Identity Accommodation in Couples

Compared to the forms of accommodation described in research on identity processes with individuals, the forms of accommodation to be described in this research on couples have a much stronger interpersonal component. In part, accommodation in the realm of relationships does involve making changes in individual identities, but it mostly involves adaptation to the nature of marriage in general, and to the partner in particular.

Two main categories of accommodation were identified in this study; one includes changes made by individuals and the second category involves changes made by both partners.

Accommodation as an individual. When there is disequilibrium between the use within a couple of assimilation and accommodation, the balance may be restored by one partner (not necessarily the one who is assimilating) taking on the role of the "accommodator." Accommodation as an individual was rated when the spouse described a one-way set of identity changes that he or she had made in response to particular experiences with the partner. No indication is given, in these descriptions, of the partner having undergone a complementary process of change.

One form of individual accommodation is behavioral adaptation to the partner's personal style or personality. The spouse tries to adapt to some characteristic of the partner in the hopes of being able to achieve greater congruence between the spouse identity and experiences within the relationship. This may take the form, for instance, of a spouse trying out the partner's method of resolving conflicts, as in this wife's response:

I try different methods of handling it because he has a shorter temper than I do so he gets angry more often, or gets upset. I've tried all kinds of things, like yelling or ignoring or not saying anything or anything I can think of, or trying to be rational.

When asked what constitutes a good relationship, she replied:

...being able to talk with each other and discuss things...maybe trying to accommodate the other one, at least sometimes, being kind to each other.

This woman's husband had not indicated that he had made changes so as to adapt to her style of resolving disputes, and therefore the process was rated as accommodation by the individual rather than the couple.

Changes in identity may or may not accompany this process of behavioral adaptation. Alterations in identity as a spouse are more likely to occur when other forms of individual accommodation are used. One of these is the adaptation to the reality of one's marital situation. This occurs when it becomes apparent to the spouse that the partner's actual characteristics do not match the spouse's initial perception of that partner or model of what kind of relationship they have. The spouse may realize, as this wife did, that the spouse is just not a very intimate person: "If he says 'I love you' then he already told me and why do I have to tell you again this month?"

The identity that emerges from this process may be "sadder but wiser," as it was for this wife:

After 11 yrs I'm still in love with him. . . . I don't always agree with him, I probably see more of his faults than I ever saw 2 years ago, not 2, let's say 10 years, even 2, yeah, and I really care about him, where he's going and I'm committed to have him find what he wants in life.

This example illustrates a healthy kind of accommodation, which has allowed for the wife to recognize discrepancies between her identity as a spouse and her partner's characteristics, and in the process preserve stability within the relationship.

Accommodation as an individual may also take the form of arriving at a changed view of oneself as a spouse. Something is lost, to be sure, when the illusions are dropped that one is a "perfect" spouse. In place of these unrealistic beliefs, though, are far more durable images of the self as one actually is in a close relationship with another person. As one wife observed, when asked to describe what constituted a good relationship, "a little bit of insight into themselves, or at least the ability to look at themselves with the other person, and understand to a certain degree."

Accommodation by an individual within the relationship may also take the form of incorporating the partner into one's own identity as a spouse. People who speak of this process refer to gradual encroachments on their sense of self as an individual in the context of the relationship:

I don't think I would be the person I am today if it weren't for him.... There's nobody that I met in my life that meets my needs and that is so my other half, my other part than he is.... I don't know if I would be interested in another relationship like this. A big whole part of me would be gone.

A husband refers to this process as more of an establishment of mutual dependence, at least from his point of view:

When you're married 10 years you start to lose a little of that independence and become dependent on somebody for something and she's my crutch and I'm her crutch for certain things.

Even if the spouse does not see the process of invasion by the partner's identity as this extreme, there is associated with this form of accommodation a movement for the spouse to see them each as becoming, in the words of one wife, "part of each other's life."

Accommodation as a couple. Couples may restore a disequilibrium to a more balanced state by accommodating their identities as spouses relative to each other. In contrast to accommodation as an individual, which leaves the identity of the nonaccommodating partner unchanged, this kind of mutual accommodation touches the identities of both spouses. They may alter their identities of themselves as intimate partners, of their model of an intimate relationship, and of their perceptions of the partner.

Logically it is possible for accommodation as a couple to take two forms. One occurs when both partners come to the realization that their relationship needs to be changed because it is no longer happy or meeting the needs of the partners, or is in some other way flawed. When this happens, both partners can be considered to be accommodating to some "absolute" standard or objective reality. This kind of accommodation was rare. Typically, the kind of accommodation observed in this study was of partners adapting to the views of each other's identities in the relationship.

Evidence for accommodation as a couple comes from descriptions by both partners of how they have changed with respect to each other. A description by only one partner of a change in behavior, perception of the relationship, or change in perception of the partner is not sufficient to qualify as mutual accommodation. Even if the spouse talks about "both" partners having made such changes, the response is not considered evidence for accommodation as a couple. Both partners must describe a similar (or complementary) process of adaptation. This is because the comments of one spouse about so-called mutual accommodation may themselves be distorted by the assimilation process. A spouse who has made heavy accommodations to the partner's identity may prefer to see this process as two-sided when in fact the sacrifices came from that spouse alone.

One kind of change that takes place through mutual accommodation is compromise by both partners of their own individual needs, interests, and preferences. In a mutually reinforcing feedback process, one person adapts to the other's needs, who in turn adapts to the other, and so on. After enough time spent in this process, neither partner can remember (or even cares) who adapted to whom. At this point, as one couple observed, they become "pretty similarly matched." No one's wishes seem to take precedence over the other because "our wishes are the same anyway." Each spouse's identity as a spouse can also change in mutually interacting ways as each learns from the other about ways to communicate and resolve conflict. Both partners adapt to each other in this process, learning to "read the signals" of each other, while at the same time teaching the partner to read one's own signals.

The mutual perception that the spouses have become interwoven in their strengths and weaknesses is another form of identity accommodation within the couple. As the result of this process, the two partners see themselves as two halves of a whole person. One couple agreed that this had happened to them over the course of their marriage. According to the husband:

I kind of look upon us as just one person. It's like the left side of the head telling the right side what's going on. It's just one organism and whichever end is closest does it. . . . Being without her would be like being without half of me . . . . I would definitely feel like I lost part of myself. Along the lines of an amputee that loses two legs or something. . . . There are skills that each of us has that the other needs. Like she has perceptual difficulties in finding her way around. I scored 99% on the Air Force navigator's test. Things that I do she can't and things that she can do and I can't.

The wife verified her husband's story:

We're almost like missing pieces of a puzzle. He's got in his head the places that are empty in mine. Like I am very strong in social skills. . . machines are a blank box to me. He takes care of all my machines. I get lost, he never gets lost.

This absorption of the partner into one's own identity as an individual is perhaps the most complete form of accommodation as a couple. The mutuality expressed by couples who describe this process approaches a "merger" (Whitbourne, 1986a) of two identities where the lines of distinction become blurred between the spouse and the partner.

Again, it must be pointed out that couples who describe this kind of mutual accommodation may be operating under a mutual illusion or myth about their relationship. Through accommodation, they may have reached a point of having merged their identities. The extent to which they actually do communicate at a high level and have established a high degree of closeness is an open question without external data. Fortunately, we were able to obtain some data pertinent to this point independently of the interview through the inclusion of a problem-solving task used for rating communciation styles of the couples.

Rating of Identity Processes in Couples

The rating of assimilation and accommodation from the self-report inter-view is a difficult and often tenuous proposition. With two self-report interviews covering the same territory, the problem is just as complicated, perhaps more so. One never knows who is "right." However, it is possible to make relative judgments of who is assimilating and who is accommoda-ting by making cross comparisons in which the rater assumes both respondents are distorting their answers. The question then becomes who is assimilating *relative* to whom (not in an absolute sense) and who seems to be doing the accommodating. For instance, a husband "overestimates" (relative to his wife) how much time the couple spends together and how much they discuss everyday affairs around the house. He may be seen to be assimilating his experiences with his wife to the belief that the couple has a close marriage. His wife may, on the other hand, see their marriage as one in which they both operate independently. Her "underestimates" will serve to confirm this belief. To the extent that people agree in their answers to questions regarding their marriage, it can be assumed that the couple share the same view of their relationship. Another way to approach to problem is to consider the case when spouses are asked how they each see some aspect of their relationship and then to say how they think their partner sees it. To the extent that spouses say the other feels the "same," or projects onto their partner the same beliefs as they have, it can be assumed that they are assimilating their view of their partner into their own view of the relationship. This logic was used to derive one of the primary measures on which the study's quantitative analyses were based.

Other ratings of assimilation and accommodation can be made by making various comparisons within each spouse's answers and by cross-checking across different answers from the two interviews. A good example of how these ratings can be made comes from the following example, taken from a couple's separate descriptions of how they met each other. The husband gave the following account:

I saw her the very first day I started my new job; we went through orientation classes together. Things were busy, so we never got together after that." Two years later, "she was standing by the side of the road . . . I picked her up and gave her a lift and nothing much came of that but later on . . . there was a bus strike and they closed the road I usually took . . . so I had to take a different route that went past her house and there she was standing on the corner waiting for the bus. I recognized those lovely legs and I circled once around the block, picked her up. That continued for the rest of the bus strike and then when the buses went rolling again we just ignored them. And the process continued from there.

His wife told the following story:

I met him soon after I started working at (name of company) and he studiously ignored me. We were in the orientation program together and I arranged to sit next to him. He didn't respond terribly well and I arranged to be walking while he was driving, but he didn't notice me so I sort of gave up on him. I really didn't have a whole lot of contact with him for the next couple of years. Then I was waiting for a bus on a cold, wet, miserable dreary day wearing what had to be one of the ugliest raincoats that was ever invented, when this car drove around and went "honk." He stopped and offered me a ride home and so I lucked out in that respect. The buses went on strike a short time later and he started picking me up and dropping me off on a regular basis.

A tip-off to something being amiss in the husband's story is his statement that he picked her up while she was waiting for a bus during a bus strike, clearly an impossibility! Her description is obviously the more accurate one from a factual standpoint. From a subjective standpoint, these stories also offer a preliminary view of what will turn out to be the framework of their relationship; namely, her identity as the "lucky" beneficiary of her husband-to-be's attention and of him as the roaming bachelor who has happened to let himself get caught by a lovely young woman. As it also turns out later in the interview, the husband leaves out a major fact about their marriage, that he is having an affair with a woman friend of the couple's. Nowhere in his interview is there even the slightest hint that this is taking place. His wife, in contrast, describes her feelings about it with a touching candor. She reluctantly goes along with his desire to "experiment," even trying to convince herself that she is happy with the uncertainty that she faces about their future together. Although she allows herself to acknowledge some of her unhappiness, she remains firmly optimistic in her attempts to assimilate her views of herself and her marriage into a favorable mold.

A final basis for making ratings of assimilation and accommodation is to compare the content of a spouse's answers with what else is known about the couple. Although based on self-report, the multiple measures used in this study provide something of a cross-check against a given set of responses to the interview. The scores and transcribed excerpts on the communication task and a questionnaire index of marital adjustment were used to define the more "objective" nature of a couple's relationship against which the spouses' responses were compared. These proved to be invaluable aids to the assessment of the identity processes as determined from the intimacy interview.

Study Methods

Sample Demographics

A group of 40 married couples served as the sample for this study. These couples were living in the greater metropolitan area of a moderate-sized Northeastern city. All couples were selected on the basis of the number of years they were married, which ranged from 5 to 20 years. Their demographic characteristics are shown in Table 1 of Appendix D. Ratings of occupation and socioeconomic status (SES) were made using the four-factor index of Hollingshead (1979). Education was rated according to number of years in school. As can be seen from the table, the sample was, on the average, college-educated and many had graduate degrees. Their occupations were, on the average, at the level of minor professional and technical workers, and this was consistent with their SES ratings. It is also clear from this table that many of the wives in this sample were employed outside the home.

For the purpose of the analyses reported in this book, the couples were divided into two groups based on the number of years they were married. The longer-married group included couples married from 11 to 20 years, and the shorter-married group contained couples married from 5 to 10 years. This division was made because 10 years was the median number of years married for the couples in the sample. Ten years also seemed to be a significant number in that a couple's 10th anniversary of marriage carries a considerable degree of symbolic meaning. The demographic characteristics of these two groups are shown at the bottom of Table 1 of Appendix D.

Procedure

Volunteers for this study were obtained from advertising in the local media of the city in which the study was conducted. As an incentive, couples were offered a booklet containing discount tickets for local restaurants and movie theaters. The couples who volunteered were screened in terms of the sampling criteria (married from 5 to 20 years, having no more than 5 children, and not in marital counseling). They were given the choice of being interviewed in their home or in the researcher's office at the university. All interviews were conducted by the second author. Prior to beginning the interview, the members of each couple read and signed a consent form. The partners were first interviewed separately; the determination of who was to be first was made randomly. While the first partner was being interviewed, the other partner completed questionnaires. After both partners were interviewed and had completed the questionnaires, they were brought together and asked to discuss three topics for five minutes apiece. These discussions were audiotaped, without the interviewer being present. The discussions were to have the following content: things that each of them did that pleased the other, coming to consensus on the Role Performance Scale (a questionnaire measure described later), and an issue or concern between the couple that had been bothering them recently. The order of the three audiotaped discussions was randomly assigned to each couple. Upon completion of this task, the couple was given a chance to comment about the research. They were then debriefed and thanked for their time. Several referrals for marital counseling were made. The entire research session took two to three hours. Two years after the study was completed, the couples were sent follow-up questionnaires asking to describe any significant changes in their lives as a couple or as individuals since the time of the study.

Intimacy Interview

The primary measure used in this research was the Adult Intimacy Interview, a modification for mature adults of the Intimacy Status Interview of Tesch and Whitbourne (1982). The interview questions are contained in Appendix A. The Intimacy Status Interview was intended for use with young adult men and women based on a version developed for college males by Orlofsky, Marcia, and Lesser (1973). Questions added for the present study to the Intimacy Status Interview concerned the sexual aspects of intimacy. These questions were adapted from Schaefer and Olson's (1981) PAIR intimacy measure.

Originally, the Adult Intimacy Interview was intended to be scored in a manner analogous to that used by Tesch and Whitbourne (1982) in the assignment of intimacy "statuses." An intimacy status was defined as a style of resolving the intimacy-versus-isolation psychosocial crisis of young adulthood, following Orlofsky et al. (1973). Scoring categories added to the original Orlofsky et al. measure were intended to reflect further complexities of male and female forms of intimacy (cf. Whitbourne, 1986a). It became evident early in scoring the interviews of the present sample of adults according to this system that the intimacy statuses had limited applicability and usefulness. Furthermore, it became evident that the intimacy statuses scoring system failed to capture the richness and complexity of the present data set, with its responses from both members of the couple. A new scoring system was therefore evolved that took into account the opportunities for comparing responses of husbands and wives to the same questions. This scoring system made possible the inferences concerning identity processes that form the basis for the results presented in this book.

The scores on which our data analyses are based were derived through a two-level process. First, the questions on the interview were coded according to the content of their responses. The coding categories used in this rating process are shown in Appendix B. Agreement on these ratings was calculated between two judges for a total of 10 interviews, and was found to average 84%. The ratings used in the study were made by the first author. Next, the coded responses were used as the basis for constructing scores representing different structural components of the interview. This scoring system is described in Appendix C.

Communication

The couple's quality of communication was rated from transcripts of the couple's five-minute discussion of a problem in the relationship. The communication rating system used was based on the Miller, Nunnally, and Wackman (1975) model. The couple's score on this measure is an index of the extent to which they use "work" styles of communication. The work styles include the use of an open style of communication in which couples are supportive, explorative, analytic, attempt to promote intimacy, express personal preferences ("I" statements), and describe their emotional experience. The "nonwork" styles include rationalizing, making idle conversation, giving information, stereotyping, bantering, joking, and the more destructive approaches of controlling, arguing, making verbal attacks, and blaming. The specific coding manual used for rating the transcript excerpts was a modification of Wampler (1979). The rating of these excerpts was conducted by four female graduate students who were extensively trained in the method. They practiced rating until they reached an 81% degree of agreement with each other and with the second author. This exceeds the 75% standard reported in other research in this area.

Marital Adjustment

The measure of marital adjustment that we used in this study was Spanier's (1976) Dyadic Adjustment Scale. This paper-and-pencil questionnaire requests respondents to rate the happiness of their present marriage as well as their feelings about other aspects of their relationship. There are 32 items on this instrument, and the range of scores it yields is from 0 to 151. The four components that make up the total score are: satisfaction, cohesion, consensus, and affection.

Egalitarianism

Couples were asked to complete a 21-item rating of the division of tasks in their relationship. The purpose of including this measure was to ascertain the contribution to total marital adjustment of couples' perceptions of the equality within their relationship. The questionnaire, called the "Role Performance Scale" had been developed by Ebmeyer (1982) in a study of dual-worker couples. The items on this questionnaire were derived from measures designed by Beckman and Houser (1979) and Perucci et al. (1978) on marital power and role allocation. Respondents were asked to rate whether each of the 21 tasks on the scale was performed more often by the husband or the wife, or whether it was performed equally. The tasks included grocery shopping, mowing the lawn, car repairs, the washing of dishes and clothes, minor household repairs, driving, shoveling snow, scrubbing floors, vacuuming the house, cleaning the bathroom, dusting furniture, cleaning drawers and closets, making the beds, deciding on which jobs each spouse takes, cleaning the refrigerator, buying presents for family members, and the planning and cooking of meals. Answers to the questions were given a score of 2 if husband and wife shared in the task equally, a score of 1 if one person generally performed the task, and a score of 0 if one person always carried out the job.

Summary of Main Findings

The main analyses of the study were conducted on quantitative measures derived from the interview. Ratings of identity assimilation and accommodation were made for the purpose of qualitative analyses of the interview transcript material. It is possible, though, to make a connection between the quantitative measures and the qualitative ratings. Identity assimilation corresponds to the quantitative measure of perceived similarity (saying that one's partner is the "same" as oneself or giving the same answer for the partner as for the self). Identity accommodation corresponds to the quantitative measure of accurate perceptions by spouses, reflecting their ability to see each other and the relationship in a relatively "objective" fashion (that is, in a manner that is in keeping with one's spouse's true perceptions).

Using these quantitative measures, separate multiple regressions were conducted for couples in the older and younger groups (according to years married). Additional predictor variables derived from the measures of communication and egalitarianism were used in these analyses. The couple's joint potential for intimacy was also used as a predictor in the multiple regressions. In all analyses, marital adjustment served as the dependent measure. Separate accounts are needed of these findings for husbands and wives, since different features of the relationship predicted their adjustment. Moreover, the regressions were separately run for couples married 10 years or less and those married 11 to 21 years. For wives, perceived similarity between spouses played a role in determining adjustment for both groups of wives. The couple's accuracy of perception did, however, also serve as a predictor of marital adjustment for the wives married over 10 years. This finding may signify that perceived similarity works for a while in promoting marital adjustment of wives, but later on real agreement is needed to maintain the wife's adjustment. Reframing this result in terms of assimilation and accommodation processes, it would appear that assimilation is a more important factor in the adjustment of wives married 10 years or less, and that over time accommodation becomes more of a factor if the wife is to remain well-adjusted. The husband's role in this process was identified in further analyses. These analyses were based on a measure derived from the interview of the "potential" for intimacy, that is, the extent to which the individual feels comfortable in exposing him- or herself to the intense emotionality of a long-term close relationship. It was found that wives married to husbands who lacked the potential to be highly intimate partners were themselves less well-adjusted in their marriage and less intimate than wives of husbands with a high potential for intimacy. Indeed, couples in which there was a highly intimate husband were better adjusted than couples in which the husband had low potential for being intimate. It may be concluded that wives will attempt to assimilate their husbands into a positive model of the relationship, at least early on in the marriage. This process is made much easier if the husband is highly intimate, since less assimilation is needed over time when he really is a "good" husband, defined by the wives in the sample as someone who is willing to help them with household tasks and who is emotionally sensitive to their needs. Husbands who lack this potential for intimacy are less easy to assimilate and, indeed, may over time have a negative effect on their wives' own willingness to be intimate with them. Wives who are married to these low intimate men have no choice eventually but to accommodate to their more negative features if the relationship is to remain intact. There was also evidence, though, for husbands, especially the highly intimate ones, accommodating to their wives over time.

For husbands, the statistical results are less clear regarding the role of assimilation and accommodation. The intimacy potential of husbands and wives served to predict the marital adjustment of men in the couples married 10 years or less. Husbands in these couples were also better adjusted if they were part of a relationship in which both partners valued good communication. For the longer-married husbands, compatibility in the area of sexuality was related to better marital adjustment. These findings are in sharp contrast to the results for wives, in that almost no weight was given to perceived similarity in the prediction of husbands' marital adjustment. It will be seen from transcript excerpts that husbands do use assimilation in viewing their relationships with their wives, but this process does not determine how well-adjusted they are. Instead, it is the couple's actual concordance in the areas of communication and sexuality that determines whether a husband is well-adjusted or not. Indeed, for husbands, there is more of a tendency to emphasize these "romantic" features of relationships compared to wives, who tend to be more down-to-earth.

The topics to be explored in depth in this book illustrate the role of identity processes in determining couples' perceptions of power dynamics, sexuality, and communication. The model of identity processes within marriage will serve as the basic framework from which these areas will be examined.

2
Identity Processes in Wives

The better-adjusted wives saw themselves and their husbands as sharing similar views of their relationships. For wives who had been married over 10 years, however, an additional factor predicting their adjustment was the actual extent of agreement between themselves and their husbands. The analyses on which these conclusions are based are reported in Table 3 of Appendix D.

A further analysis showed that the husband's potential for intimacy played a role in determining both the adjustment and intimacy potential of wives (see Table 4 in Appendix C). Wives whose husbands were low in their potential for intimacy were more likely to have lower intimacy themselves and also lower marital adjustment. Perhaps a husband who is not very intimate thus puts an undue strain on the assimilative processes of his wife. The wife eventually must give up her attempts to use assimilation and instead switch to accommodation over time. At that point, her marital satisfaction will depend less on how well she can assimilate her husband to fit her identity within the relationship and more on the husband's actual potential to be intimate.

The glimpse presented in this chapter of what the wives actually said in their interviews show that when wives use assimilation, it is to adapt the wives' perceptions of their marriages and their husbands into their spouse identity. Wives do not go out of their way to make themselves look particularly intimate or loving, but they do attempt to convince themselves that their husbands are. This is particularly true for the wives in the couples married 10 years or less. Wives in the longer-married couples are more inclined to make accommodations to adjust their identities as spouses. Here again, though, the accommodations are made in terms of the wife's perceptions of the spouse or the relationship, not in terms of the wife's own qualities as an intimate partner. The spouse identities of wives, then, are more other-oriented, both to the husband and to the model of the relationship, than we will find is true for husbands.

Couples Married 10 Years or Less

Among the wives in this group of couples are some of the most ardent believers in the "togetherness" model of marriage. This is perhaps no better exemplified than by the wife whose own body image appeared fused with that of her husband's: "We just joined the 'Y' so we'll be jogging together because we've been gaining weight together." As a group, these women are more satisfied if they and their spouse perceive there is a great deal of similarity between them, regardless of whether or not there is a basis for this perceived similarity in their actual agreement about the relationship. This process is greatly facilitated by a husband who is willing to play the role of the "companion" mate by being open, supportive, helping with the household chores, willing to make sacrifices for the wife's career (or at least share sacrifices equally), and understanding in the area of sexuality. Without such an ideal spouse, the wife must rely more on her own powers of interpretation to assimilate his actual behavior into her spouse identity.

Assimilation

Denial and assertion. Wives married 10 years or less relied heavily on this form of assimilation to "convert" their husbands so that they would be perceived as good spouses and to transform their perception of the relationship into that of a close, egalitarian one. This kind of assimilation is probably the one that accounts the most for actual disagreements between the younger husbands and wives in their descriptions of their relationship.

The most straightforward form of denial involves the wife saying that there is "no problem" in some area of their relationship when the husband clearly indicates that there is. A good illustration of this form of denial is a husband who described numerous problems and areas of dissatisfaction involving basic personality differences between himself and his wife. His wife, in contrast, maintained that: "There's no deep-seated, underlying problem, just day-to-day tired and it will relax." Other instances of denial were cases in which wives admitted that a problem existed but then minimized its seriousness, as in the following excerpt:

I usually cry and he usually pouts (laughing). No, he has the volunteer ambulance station so he can always go up there.... He might leave or his big thing is to sit two feet from the TV with his back to the rest of the living room which physically completely closes me out. I take up a book and read and take a hot bath.

The interviewer then asked if the couple talk about their disagreement at a later time. The wife responded:

If it was serious enough, but a lot of times problems just really aren't important, they're just...after that night they're gone and not really worth it.

After describing what might be regarded as a fairly serious limitation in the couple's method of handling disagreements, the wife then denies that something is wrong by claiming that the problems are not "serious enough" to talk about.

Assertion as a counterpart of denial accounted for many of the instances of presumed similarity in the responses to the intimacy interview questions, that is, the spouse insisting that the partner feels the "same" as the spouse on a particular issue. This type of response formed the basis for the presumed similarity score derived from the intimacy interview. For wives married 10 years or less, in particular, this kind of assimilation as used by both partners was highly predictive of marital adjustment. Assertion by the wives in this group also took the form of the wife's claiming that the couple discussed such diverse features of their relationship as finances, household chores, and feelings, and the husband saying that they did not. The discrepancy between spouses could be seen in some couples as the contrast between the wife's belief that she was "discussing" (i.e., talking) something over with her husband and his description of himself as a passive listener. In one couple, for example, the husband said that, regarding finances, "she discusses them with me, but I don't discuss them with her." The wife, in contrast, asserted that "mostly we discuss them." To admit that her husband was not a participant in this discussion would be to challenge this wife's identity as a spouse married to a husband who is able to discuss issues of importance to the couple.

A more complicated form of assertion was seen in the case of another couple regarding the issue of how much time they spent together. It was the husband's view that the couple had little free time together. From the wife's perspective:

There's not defined free time. I wouldn't say we get home at 5 and we're together until the next morning every day. In a way all our time is free time, but we choose to fill it and we fill it with job or with the kids or with something we want to do.

By redefining what is customarily meant by "free time," the wife was able to assert that what was admittedly less than ample time together really was sufficient.

An interesting combination of denial and assertion as forms of assimilation could be seen in the responses of some wives to the question of how they and their partners would react to a dissolution of the relationship. The belief that their husbands would be more devastated than they conflicted sharply with the responses of the husbands that they would definitely survive, if not prosper. In one couple, the husband even went so far as to admit that he had fantasies about "what a nice life" he would have if their relationship ended. His wife was secure in her belief that he would "fall apart" if their relationship were to come to an end, although she qualified this prediction by suggesting that perhaps he would just "cry inside."

Denial and assertion as assimilative tactics used by wives to maintain a positive identity about themselves in their relationships are required more in couples where the husband is low in his own potential for intimacy.

Indeed, the examples just cited were taken from couples in which the husband's self-intimacy score was well below the midpoint of the group. The wives with husbands whose intimacy was high had less of a need to distort their perceptions of the relationship. These husbands were far more amenable to the kind of closeness that fit the spouse identities of the wives as being involved in a very intimate relationship. One wife whose husband fit this description seemed herself to have considerable insight into how she had assimilated this feature of their experiences as a couple to her identity as a spouse. She first defined a good relationship as involving:

...trust, good communication...an understanding of the other person's goals and beliefs...Enjoyment of the other individual, same sense of humor.

When asked how much of this she felt that they had obtained, she replied: "Since I selected the variables, I think we've attained those!" A husband who believes that intimacy is important and who is reasonably able to follow through on this belief in his behavior, is one who is relatively easy for a wife to assimilate into her identity as a spouse in a romantic marriage.

However, there were some exceptions. One came from a couple in which the husband, though his intimacy potential was high, appeared to be trying to extricate himself from the overly romantic model to which his wife was trying to make him conform. Throughout their interview were instances of his attempts to define himself more independently from his wife and their relationship. The following excerpt illustrates one of the most discrepant pairs of responses to the same question in the entire study and shows clearly the wife's use of assertion to validate the view that they had an authentic "togetherness" form of marriage. According to the husband, what this couple does in their free time is:

On the weekends, it's hectic because we have to do everything that can be done on the weekend, and that involves visiting friends, visiting relatives, which are one hour away or five hours away, so our weekends are usually consumed spending our time with other people.

The wife portrayed the following image of their free time together:

On the weekends we try and get all our things that need to be done done and we have a stamp collection and we take photographs, we just go for a drive, go for a walk, go to a mall, a lot of things where we can just be alone and talk or just do a lot of quiet things. A lot of times we just sit and talk. It's nice to just sit and talk.

One can hardly believe that this couple are describing the same marriage! However, the wife's account is consistent with many of her other descriptions throughout the interview of just how close they are, descriptions that contrast sharply with her husband's more qualified analyses of the extent of togetherness in their marriage. She regards him as the most important thing in her life; in contrast, he sees her as important to him as his work. She thinks about him "all the time," he thinks about her a couple of hours a day, on and off. The wife seemed not to have received her husband's messages that he would like more room to maneuver in the relationship. Of course, the picture is not entirely negative from her husband's point of view, and he did say that he appreciates how "outgoing" she is. Nor is intimacy something that he eschews. He did receive a high score on the intimacy questions (as high as his wife's) and he says, at least, that being able to talk is important to a good relationship. This is what makes it relatively easy for his wife to assimilate him to her own model of their "romantic" marriage.

Justification of spouse's behavior. Wives using this form of assimilation gave excuses for their husband's failure to fit their own spouse identity regarding what an ideal husband should be in an ideal type of relationship. A wife might attribute her husband's low intimacy to his upbringing, to his being busy with work, or to her own shortcomings. In this way, her perception of her husband's behavior could still be fit into her own identity as a spouse married to an intimate man despite his obvious lack of enthusiasm for the idea of togetherness and good communication in marriage.

In this next excerpt, the wife defended her husband's inability to establish closeness with her on the basis of personality traits that were, presumably, beyond his control to change:

He's different than I am, I think he's more introverted than I am and maybe he needs me as a comforter sometimes, like a baby blanket I suppose. But I'm there even though he just wants to sit around and hang on.

Not only did this wife manage to attribute her husband's reluctance to be intimate to his personality, but in the same breath she concludes that underneath it all, he really does need her.

Use of other-justification was also found in the responses of wives married to men with high potential for intimacy. The wife, quoted earlier, whose romantic portrayal of their weekend activities differed so strikingly from her husband's, accounted for his lack of helpfulness around the house in the following manner:

There are times when if I'm doing the dishes and the household type things, I guess it's natural for me to think that we would split everything 50–50, but it doesn't happen because he's so busy and he's got other things that he's working toward another goal. I guess it's natural for me at times to feel a little resentful. If that's the case, I try to do something else rather than bring it out because I know there is nothing that he can really do about it. It's not his fault.

This woman admits to being resentful, but quickly covers it over by justifying her husband's behavior as due to situational rather than underlying personality attributes. Other wives in younger couples saw their husband's lapses from a romantic model of a relationship as due to their being "men", who are biologically programmed not to share their feelings. One wife expressed a great deal of resentment toward her husband's lack of understanding in the sexual domain, but regarded this as due to the fact that men are all "sexual animals." She wistfully muses: "I wish there were more excitement. TV and these books I read, they make it sound like something hot." By chalking her sexual disappointment off to characteristics that he has no control over (i.e., that he is male), she can exonerate him from blame over his failure to satisfy her more completely. Given her belief that her husband does his "best" under these circumstances, and her satisfaction with his efforts to "spoil" her in other areas of their relationship, she is able to avoid letting these problems with their relationship detract from her favorable spouse identity.

External projection of problems. Individuals often project onto other people or circumstances the blame for the difficulties that beset them. This kind of projection alleviates the guilt, shame, and distress that individuals would otherwise face if they had to admit to a flaw in themselves as the cause of the problem. In the case of individuals, this is a form of assimilation that people use to protect their own identities. In the case of a married couple, the attribution of the cause of problems to factors outside the couple serves a similar purpose of protecting the spouse identities of the partners. It therefore can be seen as a form of assimilation. It is of course possible that outside influences can interfere with what is otherwise a good relationship and that the wives who attribute their marital distress to these outside influences are being accurate rather than using assimilation. However, it can also be argued that a well-adjusted couple will resolve these problems successfully and may even feel that they profit by them, presenting a united front against adversity.

The wife in one of the most poorly adjusted couples in the sample (who divorced less than two years after the study was completed), relied very heavily on external projection. She believed that the reason she and her husband did not interact as often as she would like was because of the interference of the children:

The children is the modifying factor in terms of not putting the number of extra hours in or the trips or whatever we would have done had we been single or without children. . . . I think we basically have a good relationship, but it's made stormy by the children, by work, by all those kinds of qualifying things which are putting a lot of demands on the situation, which is sometimes difficult to deal with.

This woman attributed her lack of closeness with her husband, whose intimacy score is very low, to the fact that they have so many "nitty gritty" issues confronting them as a couple. With other people, she has been able to be share more "interpersonally" because "you could go home to your own house and meditate and withdraw and not have to deal with these other issues."

Major flaws in a relationship due, at least in part, to the husband's low potential for intimacy, can thus be written off with this mode of assimilation to other causes. In this way, the wife can still manage to see the "basic" relationship (without these interferences) as one that is fundamentally healthy.

Idealization of spouse. Only among couples in which the husbands had high potential for intimacy was this mode of assimilation observed. The wife who relies on idealization as a means of assimilating her experiences in the relationship into her identity as a spouse portrays her partner as flawless, and as someone she must, perforce, regard with awe. As expressed by this wife, her husband is the height of perfection:

I absolutely revere and admire him. I feel he's a truly gifted person and I feel that he is my best friend as well as my lover and just everything. He's everything to me. He's really my world...as far as sharing this kid, and he's been an absolutely wonderful, wonderful father. Very attentive, changing diapers, everything right down the line. He's been a very good support system for me, through this.

Her efforts to assimilate her husband's personality and behavior into this ideal image are not totally without basis, as he does seem to at least reciprocate her feelings toward him of regarding each other as best friends and being very much in love. It is likely that she exaggerated the extent of his help to her, given that he says that "she is doing more of the household type things, just because she seems to have more time."

This husband did seem fairly amenable, though, to taking on his share of the child-care role. To a certain extent, he supported her model of their relationship as an exceptionally close one, but he held back from completely giving in to it. He described the relationship as "one of the most important things in my life"; for her it is "paramount." He did not spend much time thinking about the relationship; what he did think about were the "maintenance" aspects "rather than thinking about is this a good relationship, is this a bad relationship." In contrast, she spent considerable time "questioning and reviewing things for myself and thinking ahead and thinking about him and ways to make an even good thing better." He said it is better not to share everything (e.g., old girlfriends and "transient emotions, when something goes wrong"); she would share everything with him. Perhaps the biggest divergence in viewpoints between this husband and wife about the nature of their relationship is one that she has not yet had to confront. Her husband expressed the fear that his wife, who took a maternity leave from her job, might decide to go back to work in the near future. This would place more demands on him to help at home, an obligation that he resists because: "I have managed to get myself a job which is very demanding on my time and very rigid as far as its demands on my time." His wife, however, is operating under the assumption that her egalitarian husband will of course support her desire to return to work: "He will say: 'I'll take care of the family, you need to get out.'" Although true that this husband, with his high potential for intimacy, is easily transformable into the ideal mate, he does have clay feet, which his wife's assimilation does not allow her to see.

Accommodation

The accommodation to husbands by wives married 10 years or less differed considerably according to whether their husbands were high or low in their potential for intimacy. A husband who is truly incapable of participating in a close relationship with a high degree of sharing presents a real challenge for a wife to assimilate into her identity as a spouse in a relationship characterized by togetherness. As earlier examples showed, it is technically possible to assimilate into a favorable spouse identity the husband whose potential for intimacy is low, but over time the disequilibrium that this situation creates will become too unstable to be maintained. If the relationship is to survive, the wife must at that point accommodate her identity to take into account her husband's actual limitations. Examples of accommodation as an individual show the extent to which wives will alter their behavior, views of themselves, and views of their husbands and the relationship to adapt to nonintimate husbands whose positions in the relationship remain immutable.

Some wives whose husbands have low potential for intimacy attempted to tailor their own behavior to compensate for their husband's limitations. They might develop an increased sensitivity to their husband's moods, as was the case in this couple: "She's gotten to the point where she knows what's bothering me and how to correct it before I even say anything."

The danger of this kind of accommodation is that by becoming so tuned in to her husband's emotional cues, the wife reduces his motivation to learn how to express himself more openly. A wife with a low-intimacy husband might also learn to circumvent areas in which he is particularly sensitive and thus reluctant to open up to her. She might find soothing or at least non-irritating ways to approach him concerning these difficult issues. One husband admitted that he was sensitive to his wife's rejecting his sexual advances. His wife's accommodation to this characteristic of his is apparent in her observation that, with regard to initiating sexual relations:

There's always the element that you have to worry about the feeling of rejection. So it's real important as to how it's brought up and when and all that.

The wife, by adapting her response to take into account her husband's sensitivities, allows him to feel less anxious but also makes it less likely that he himself will accommodate to her in the future.

Accommodation by a wife to a low-intimacy husband can, over time, have serious drawbacks stemming in part from the one-sidedness of the changes she makes. The more she accommodates to her husband, the less he is stimulated to change his identity as a spouse, and the more the wife is forced to use individual accommodation on subsequent occasions in order to adapt to his characteristics. The more extreme the imbalance between the partners becomes, the more likely it is that the wife will give up the struggle and revert to less-intimacy-enhancing forms of individual accommodation. As the realization sinks in that her husband simply is not an intimate person and probably never will be, she may find herself "burned out" trying to adapt to him. A wife in a relationship characterized by very low marital adjustment in both partners talked at length about this process:

He'll come home at night and he's had a bad day. I try real hard to be supportive and not to start picking on him or demanding his attention. He likes to be left alone when he's having a hard time and after six years I'm finally learning ways to leave him alone without feeling hurt and going crying in a corner. . . . I try to get him to talk about it but I'm not sure he likes that.

A key to what might happen in the future for this couple comes from her observation that:

I've learned that if it's something that no human being can do for me, that I have to do it myself and that's taken a lot too, to learn that he can't do for me what I have to do for myself. . . . I think we just need to continue. . . learning to live as individuals instead of this idealistic couple.

It is probably inevitable that in time she will grow away from him as her model of an intimate relationship changes to take into account the reality of her situation. A further step away would be for her to set her sights elsewhere as far as finding an intimate companion. Some wives had already made this move, turning to their family or friends as substitutes for husbands with whom they could not share their feelings and ideas. What can be seen happening, then, in the case of wives married to husbands with low potential for intimacy, is a downward spiral of movement towards lower and lower levels of intimacy within the relationship as a whole.

More neutral forms of accommodation were also observed among the wives in this group, as in the case of a wife who had changed her attitude toward spending money as the result of exposure to her husband's behavior:

I would say I've changed some and decided that his point of view is worth at least accepting some of the time. . . that certain things just aren't that important to him, then maybe they shouldn't be that important to me.

This kind of change does not seem to have the potential to establish an unstable imbalance between assimilation and accommodation within the couple and, indeed, might even be a necessary corrective in order to maintain the smooth functioning of this marriage.

Individual accommodation on the part of wives married to men with high potential for intimacy takes a much more positive course than in couples with low-intimacy husbands. In these situations, the husband is already well able to communicate his needs and feelings and so misunderstandings are less likely to occur. Furthermore, high-intimacy husbands behave in ways that more nearly approach the ideal models that the younger wives seem to have of how a husband should behave in a close relationship. When the wife accommodates to such a husband, she does not feel that she is making undue sacrifices.

The attention and interest that a husband with a high potential for intimacy may show his wife can enhance her identity as a spouse through the favorable attention provided by her husband's concern for her. A clear example of this came from one couple in which the husband made frequent reference to his greater attachment to and dependence on his wife, to the point that he becomes distraught if she has to leave him even for a short period of time. In her words:

I've had very few business trips but the times I've been away for a night or two he's at odds, he doesn't know what to do. He wanders around, watches terrible television shows and calls everyone he knows.

He is not pleased with but has gotten used to the idea of her spending time on her hobbies that take her outside the home. He said that in the past:

I used to perceive a lot of things that she did separately from me as a threat or as an indication that she preferred something to being with me and I didn't like that.

The dependence this man shows on his wife is translated into continuing efforts on his part to court her, as he said:

I think what we need to do is keep paying attention to each other. We are both very immersed in our careers and what we're each doing individually and we're both getting older and more complacent with one another as well. Sexually and romantically and in every respect I think we both need to just keep paying attention, to keep it fresh, to keep it new.

His wife saw no significant problems in their relationship and, indeed, was very content with their marriage. This is understandable, given that her husband's desire to hold onto his wife probably translated into attentive behaviors directed toward her that bolster her identity.

A wife can also benefit from her marriage to a husband high in intimacy capacity through learning how to be more effective at implementing her own identity as a spouse in an open and loving relationship. Furthermore, a husband high in intimacy potential models or even directly teaches the kinds of self-disclosing behaviors and constructive ways of resolving conflict that are likely to promote harmonious interactions within the relationship, as in the following excerpts from statements by wives:

I used to be extremely quiet and withdrawn, but now I just sit down for a few seconds to try and sort out something so I say something in a rational manner and try and get it out, when you do this I feel this way or, this is how I see it and obviously we're not seeing it the same way and I really fear that if we don't do this, this will happen. In the first few years of marriage I would just pout and go into my room and wait for him to come in and find out what was troubling me. And he wouldn't come in. So that ended that game very quickly.

This wife, then, was able to respond to her husband's efforts to change her behaviors in an indirect way. For another wife, the process was more direct:

I'm the quiet type. He will recognize that and take the initiative and say what's wrong, I think we need to talk. So he picks up on my nonverbal signals.

In contrast to the downward spiral that occurs when wives must accommodate to husbands with low intimacy potential, the process of individual accommodation under these circumstances should have a much more favorable outcome in terms of promoting the bonds between partners. Presumably, after learning from their husbands ways to interact more effectively, more mutual processes of identity change will naturally develop.

Couples Married Longer Than 10 Years

Wives in the longer-married couples, like their counterparts married 10 years or less, were better adjusted if they were in marriages characterized by a high degree of perceived similarity between husband and wife. There was a major difference, however, between the wives in these two groups of couples in the extent to which accuracy of perceptions by husband and wife predicted marital adjustment. For wives in the longer-married couples only, high accuracy was a predictor of marital adjustment. This finding suggests that these wives rely partly on assimilation, but also upon accommodation in achieving a high level of functioning within the marriage.

Assimilation

Denial and assertion. This form of assimilation was used by longer-married wives in ways comparable to the wives married 10 years or less. The longer-married wives minimized the apparent existence of problems and magnified the extent of agreement and discussion in ways that closely paralleled the statements of younger women. One woman married to a man whose potential for intimacy was low, for instance, asserted that they talk "more than ever" about their relationship. Her assessment contrasted sharply with that of her husband, who maintained that they do not talk about their feelings very often: "Because of the military I've learned to dissociate work from house and as such I've probably buried a lot of my feelings."

Compared to wives married 10 years or less, though, wives in the longer-married couples relied less heavily on denial and assertion as assimilative tactics. Even when they did so, they presented a less cheery and optimistic view of their identities as spouses than did wives in the younger couples. One wife observed, for instance, that if she and her husband separated, she would be inconvenienced because it took her a long time to "break him in" (hardly a glowing description but positive nevertheless). However, from everything else said in the interview, he truly did not appear to have been "broken in" very much at all. With low intimacy potential, he was not particularly involved in the companionship elements of their relationship. They were having unresolved, chronic disagreements about where to live, and according to her, "every time I bring that up he says he's not moving and tells me to go ahead if I want to." Despite all their difficulties, though, she insisted on seeing their relationship as growing: "I think like all relationships it continues to grow and there's always some places that need work but that's just part of being alive." Even this assertion that things are really all right between them has, compared to assimilative statements by younger wives, a much more realistic component ("there's always some places that need work").

Another example illustrating how wives married longer than 10 years differ from the shorter-married wives in their use of assimilation comes from a couple in which the husband, who has low intimacy potential, described himself as able only to "think" but not to "feel". He admitted to being "more demonstrative than you might think," but still maintained the position that he was basically a nonintimate person (his identity as a spouse will be explored in the following chapter). Despite his protestations, his wife asserted that she believed he "feels" the same about her as she does about him, and that "we do discuss our feelings." These assertions are not unilateral, though, and she did seem to have accommodated to the fact that he basically is not a warm and cuddly person and never will be. She admits that they do not talk about their feelings "as often as I think I'd like to," and that although he is not as demonstrative as she would like him to be, "we kind of complement each other." This tinge of realism, along with the idea of balance, suggests that some features of her husband's identity as a spouse have penetrated her own ideas about the relationship.

Justification of spouse's behavior. Wives in the longer-married couples tend more to blame themselves in the process of justifying the less-than-desirable features of the behaviors and personalities of their husbands. Examples of this form of assimilation were found only among wives married to men with high intimacy potential. It is possible that wives of men whose intimacy is low eventually despair of trying to justify their husband's aloofness and turn instead to other modes of adaptation. Conversely, wives of men with high intimacy potential may find their situation generally so positive that any defects in it must, they reason, be due to limitations in themselves. One wife, whose own intimacy potential was relatively low, noted that it is she who is at fault when they have disagreements, that she is the one who gets "uptight about too many things," and "over-reacts":

I'll try to think, he's not doing what he should be doing because he's a very casual person and the fault may not be his, it might be my own fault.

Taking this process one step further, some wives with high-intimacy husbands turned self-blame into projected "blame-from-other." This kind of convoluted assimilation takes the form of the wife thinking that her husband is dissatisfied with her for some quality that she is dissatisfied with in herself. For instance, one wife noted that in disagreements:

I'll clam up and he's pretty calm...he just says what's bothering him and I will clam up for a short time and then say something.... He would probably rather than I not clam up like that when I do.

Her husband never mentioned this supposed quality of hers as a problem at all; indeed, he described the main problem in their relationship as one of figuring out how better to coordinate their career goals. In another longer-married couple, both spouses blamed themselves for their marital difficulties. The husband believed it was his bringing problems home from work that caused their arguments: "I vent those frustrations at home and I know it's no good, but it's a way I deal with things." The wife, for her part, maintained they fight about "a couple of petty little things that I pick on." What is interesting about this example is that it contrasts with instances of self-blame by wives observed in the couples married 10 years or less. Wives in the shorter-married group whose husbands had a high potential for intimacy tended to blame themselves rather than their husbands for problems within the marriage and thus leave unscathed their husband's favorable image. In this longer-married couple, in contrast, the husband and wife both were willing to excuse their partner for whatever deficiencies existed in their relationship. As will be seen later, mutual willingness by both partners to accommodate through compromise was a crucial feature in determining the adjustment of longer-married couples; in some ways this sharing of blame for marital difficulties can be seen as a special variant of that process.

External projection of problems. For obvious reasons, a main difference between couples married 10 years or less compared to longer-married couples is in the age of their children. The wives in the shorter-married couples were coping with the transition to parenthood and the demands of raising young children. Most of the couples married over 10 years were freed from these burdens, but were more tied down by commitments outside the home through their children's extracurricular interests. As with the shorter-married couples, though, if the partners were well-adjusted within their relationship, the requirements of child-rearing tended not to be seen as detracting from their identities as spouses.

   The potential exists, though, for a couple's marital adjustment to suffer independently by virtue of the fact that couples do have less time together than they otherwise might like even if they both have the potential to be intimate. For one couple in which both partners had high intimacy scores (and high communication as well), the wife's marital adjustment was low due to what her husband noted was lack of

quality time...it's so easy to get caught up in spending the time doing other things...we have to schedule time to spend with each other and if you don't do that, it's easy for the relationship to deteriorate.

The wife observed that "it seems to me like we talked about more important things before we got married than after we got married." Both seemed to regret the imposition of outside time demands on what is otherwise, they believe, a good relationship. Diametrically opposed to this couple was another in which both partners had low intimacy potential (and low communication) and the wife had a high marital adjustment score. She felt that the reason they did not think much about their relationship was because there were "so many other things happening that we really don't spend a lot of time thinking about it." The difference between these two couples is instructive. The first, with high potential for intimacy and good communication, is frustrated from fulfilling their potential identities as spouses within the relationship due to time constraints that appear to keep them from spending as much time as they would like together. This couple might, it could be argued, be a later version of some of the couples married less than 10 years whose togetherness model of a relationship had been easily fulfilled since they had no children to distract them from each other. The second couple lacked potential for a close relationship, but maintained their identities as spouses in a good marriage by attributing their problems to external factors. Again, as with the shorter-married couples, children (or other commitments that compete for time with marriage) serve as a convenient assimilative vehicle for a nonintimate couple to maintain their identities as spouses who would be close if they only had the chance. As we shall see in Chapter 7, however, it is possible that these two couples are more alike than not. Couples may invent many outside "commitments" for the sake of being able to preserve their identities as close and loving spouses whose lack of closeness is due to forces outside their control. If the first couple really wanted to have more time together, chances are that such time could be found.

Accommodation

Wives married more than 10 years to husbands with low potential for intimacy tend, as shown earlier, to be better adjusted if they mix their more biased assimilative perceptions with more realistic ones based on accommodation. As with the wives married 10 years or less, the outcome of the accommodation process depends heavily on the intimacy potential of the husband.

For the most part, there is a negative long-term effect on a wife's favorable identity as a spouse when she is married to a man whose capacity for intimacy is limited. The wife of the husband with the lowest intimacy score found, for instance, that the best way to help him at busy times was to stay out of his way, a situation he prefers because "there isn't time...and I don't think she has the technology for some things." He defers from sharing his worries and problems with her "because she wouldn't understand." Correspondingly, his wife reported that when she sees their monthly funds running low, "I get nervous and jerky about that and when I talk to him about it, sometimes he doesn't want to hear about it and I get angry about that." Over time, she has responded to her husband's reluctance to share things by learning to draw a line on how much she will share with him. In the process, she finds that she no longer "idolizes him" the way she had before. She has also turned to sources of support outside the marriage:

I think people need a lot of support and I think one of the reasons that young marriages get into trouble is that each spouse looks to the other for everything. There is absolutely no way that he could meet all my needs and there's no way that I can meet all his needs. If I foolishly thought that I could and he got them met elsewhere that would set me up to be hurt.

In this response can be seen a continuation of the process observed in the wives married 10 years or less who had begun to move away from their husbands after prolonged efforts to accommodate to their low intimacy.

Accommodation by the wife to a husband with low intimacy potential need not always have the effect of interfering with the wife's marital adjustment or lowering her own potential for intimacy. The wife may find fulfillment in adapting to her husband's identity as a spouse if this is consistent with her own view of how a relationship should be. The best example of this process comes from a wife married to a man who clearly regarded himself as the decision maker and correctly perceived that his wife thinks so too: "Her feeling is that if I wanted to go left and she knew left was absolutely wrong we would go left." This situation came about, the husband maintained, because his own father was "head of the house," and because "the Bible says who heads the house." His wife agreed that he is "head of the house," and gives the reason as being:

I think he came from a patriarchal situation . . . and that's basically what we have in our home. . . . My father had died when I was an infant. That was what I wanted in a family.[1] And also we're both Christians and it's backed up in scripture that the husband should be the head of the house. I have no problem with that.

It is not clear from her response whether she sought a man who would make up for what she felt she lacked while growing up or whether she has adapted through accommodation to his model of a relationship. In either case, her situation illustrates that although married to a man with low intimacy potential, a wife might achieve high marital adjustment through a process of accommodating to the husband's desires in the relationship. She can thus maintain a favorable identity as a spouse, since she sees herself in the kind of relationship that she says she prefers.

As observed with the wives married under 10 years, marriage to a man with high potential for intimacy can have a powerful facilitative effect on a woman's identity as a spouse. Through her husband's consistently en-

---

[1] This was the respondent's actual statement; it represents an interesting slip of the tongue, perhaps.

couraging his wife to be more intimate, a wife in this situation experiences almost daily reinforcement of her own favorable identity as a spouse. As expressed by one wife:

I don't know if it's conscious on his part, I don't expect it is because he's a romantic, and I know, many times if we're going to go out I just think he looks so nice and I will just take time to say "You look really terrific." When I get dressed in the morning and I'm off to work, he'll say "that really looks good on you." We talk about our physical attractiveness to each other.

What is interesting in this wife's response is how his "romantic" attention to her appearance has, apparently, taken hold in the way she relates to her husband. Indeed, he himself claims to feel toward her "a high degree of respect; proud of the fact that even after many years of the other stresses in our lives, she is still wife, lover."

Other wives whose husbands have high intimacy potential make similar observations about the effect of their husband's interest in the relationship on their identities as spouses. What is important to one wife about their relationship is:

Love, his support for me, his need for me.... He likes to be protective towards me. He likes to be able to support me and the children. He likes my body, he told me.

To another wife, it is that:

He's everything, he's very supportive of me, he's very tuned in to my emotions. He can tell when something just isn't right, when I clam up.

One can also sense in these excerpts the receptiveness that the wives in these couples have to being encouraged to be more intimate by their husbands. This observation reinforces the finding that the intimacy potential of husbands is a more important influence on the marital adjustment of wives than the intimacy of wives is on the adjustment of husbands. Apparently, wives are in general more "primed" to having their intimacy enhanced by their partners. If their husband has high intimacy potential, even wives who are low in intimacy will respond by accommodating to the efforts of their husbands. For example, one wife whose own intimacy potential was low, found herself surprised by how much her husband, a highly intimate man, had become a part of her identity:

I don't have that many opportunities to get away by myself. Last week, for example, I was asked to a national conference in Chicago, and for me that doesn't happen too often and for me it was a big deal and I wanted him to come with me, but he was unable to. I went on my own and had a good time, but I kept thinking, gee, he would have enjoyed this meal so much, or he would have enjoyed this so much, but it won't be the same as if he had been there. I think I'm very wrapped up in him maybe even more than I realize.

This wife had come to take her husband's continuous presence for granted so that it was not until they were separated that she realized the extent to which she had come to incorporate him into her own identity.

There is, it should be noted, a potential risk that a wife runs in becoming so heavily sold on her husband's model of a relationship. This risk can be seen in the following excerpt:

He has such strong feelings on everything. His identity is so strong that sometimes I have to say, you have to know when your identity has to just stay with you and not pull me into it. In some ways I want to find out what I am without that shadow there.

A wife may have to pull back deliberately, pull away from the temptation to follow her husband's lead in establishing the emotional over- and undertones of the relationship. Otherwise she may lose her identity, not only as a spouse but as an individual, as it threatens to become submerged into that of her husband.

In general, then, the accommodation of wives to their husbands would seem to represent an attempt by wives to adjust their own intimacy levels to match that of their husbands more closely. In the process, the spouse identities of wives become increasingly refined to match the model of intimacy to which their husbands ascribe. We shall look next at the husbands to observe the assimilation and accommodation processes that complement these adaptive efforts of their wives.

3
Identity Processes in Husbands

The main difference observed between husbands and wives in the statistical analyses was that, for husbands, perceived similarity between spouses was not predictive of marital adjustment. The actual qualities of the relationship between the two partners determined the marital adjustment of husbands. For the husbands married 10 years or less, the potential of both partners for intimacy predicted marital adjustment (see Table 3 in Appendix D). Furthermore, husbands in longer-married couples were more satisfied if they and their wives agreed that each was sexually satisfied in the marriage (see Table 6 in Appendix D).

These results do not imply that husbands use no assimilation in the perception of their experiences within the relationship. Husbands do use assimilation, but to different ends than do wives. When husbands assimilate their experiences in the marriage, they do so for the purpose of maintaining a consistent view of themselves as spouses. This is perhaps why assimilation plays such a central role in the marital adjustment of wives. They adjust better to their marriage if they can transform their perception of their relationship and their husband so that it is consistent with their identities as wives in "good" relationships married to "good" husbands (defining "good" in a manner based on their personalities and experiences). The assimilation used by husbands is less interactive and more individualistic. Husbands try to "remake" or fit into their identities their perceptions of themselves, not their perceptions of their relationships or their wives. This difference may reflect sex-role socialization processes in which men learn to be self- and women to be other-directed.

Before jumping too heartily on the bandwagon of gender differences in basic personality orientations, however, it is important to point out the importance of individual variations within genders. Not factored into the statistical prediction of marital adjustment, but important in contributing to group differences, was the husband's potential to be intimate in a close relationship. The index of intimacy potential was found to differentiate sharply the adjustment of their wives. Evidence concerning identity processes in husbands will continue to reinforce the importance of considering this individual difference variable as a contributor to the marital adjustment of both spouses.

Couples Married 10 Years or Less

Interpretation of the comments made by husbands in these couples suggests that husbands retain in their identities as spouses for at least the first 10 years of marriage some very adolescent fantasies about close relationships. Husbands are preoccupied with romance and keeping the "flames of love" alive. Wives, in contrast, seem to accommodate to the everyday mundane features of marriage much earlier in their adult lives, so that by the time they were studied here they no longer gave much indication of operating according to such a model. This presents a surprising reversal of the "his and her marriage" reported by Bernard (1973), in which husbands were more preoccupied with practical matters and wives with romantic notions. The men in our sample had their heads in the clouds of passion and love, while their wives had their feet firmly planted in the ground of married life and its associated chores and duties.

Assimilation

In contrast to the kind of assimilation shown by wives married 10 years or less, the assimilation used by husbands is much more focused on their own performance as spouses. Wives, it will be recalled, directed their assimilation outward, toward portraying more favorable views of their husbands and the relationship than was probably justified. The assimilation of husbands was more self-directed, both in terms of seeing themselves as the center of the relationship and as the prime instigators of positive developments within the relationship. To a certain extent, this kind of "egocentrism" is an accurate reflection of the fact that the intimacy level of husbands was a key factor, both direct and indirect, in determining the marital adjustment of wives. Furthermore, the husbands may be convinced that they are better spouses than they are because they have been the target of assimilation on the part of their wives, who are attempting to enhance their own spouse identities by perceiving their spouses in a more favorable light. Wives may also deliberately protect their husbands, especially if their husbands seem to be reasonably good partners, from learning about any problems that the wives may be experiencing. One husband, for instance, believed that their relationship was on "an even keel." This belief seemed to prevent his wife from sharing with him "some things I don't think he could fully comprehend." Thus, the assimilation used by husbands may reflect less of a motivated effort to arrive at a favorable identity as a spouse and more a reflection of the identity processes that wives use to enhance the identities of their husbands.

In general, though, husbands whose intimacy potential was high tended to use assimilation to protect and preserve an ideal image of themselves as spouses. They viewed themselves as highly romantic husbands whose main purpose in life was to make their wives happy through focusing on love, harmony, and togetherness. To talk about the everyday necessities of life would detract from their identities as the Prince Charming in their marriage. Thus, the focus of these men in their answers to questions about the relationship was on love, maintaining harmony, and interjecting excitement into their everyday lives with their wives. One of the most extreme cases was that of the husband who had encouraged his wife to seek an open marriage, an idea that his wife found very disturbing but agreed to in order to please her husband. The husband gave no indications of his wife's unhappiness. Instead, he described himself in terms that reinforce his identity as the ideal husband. The relationship, he says is:

a number-one priority almost 100% of the time. When it slips from that it's an unconscious sort of thing, obviously pressures of the job and so forth, you put it aside out of your consciousness. It's always there, it's a given. I don't have to worry about that, solid rock, but just by the fact that we do recognize that it is such a nucleus around which everything revolves.

He and his wife, he says, talk a great deal about their relationship, although this has diminished over the course of time: "It's obviously something you're very conscious of in year one and it probably decays naturally." However, he claimed not to take the relationship for granted. He tries to keep the intimacy level high by working at it, he said, and when reflecting on how much of a good relationship they have attained, feels that it is:

...a high degree, we've had to work...when you take the time to step back and look at the whole scheme of a lifespan and say this is what it's all about and we remind ourselves that therefore we ought to work at it the way you work at a job...we aren't able to do it all the time, but it is a conscious thought frequently to say we'd better work at it.

It is a testimonial to the power of assimilation that this husband could believe that he is as good a husband as he implied, unless, of course, he is deliberately covering up the problems in the relationship. At the same time, though, it is true that his wife was busily assimilating her perceptions of him into her identity as a spouse in a good marriage. Consequently, he had no reason to doubt that she was satisfied and could therefore ignore the discrepancies between his view of himself as a devoted husband, and his behavior of engaging in an extramarital relationship over and above his wife's objections.

The group of husbands high in intimacy potential, it will be recalled, tended to be idealized by their wives and excused from any flaws that they might show from time to time. What mattered most to the wives, though, was not the quality of their husbands as lovers, but the quality of their husbands as mates and companions. Apparently, a husband who talks about the importance of love and romance in defining his own identity as a spouse is easily assimilated by his wife into her own model about what constitutes a good spouse and an ideal relationship. At least for the wives married 10 years or less, a husband who claims to be a romantic is seen as one who performs more equitably around the house as well. From the husband's point of view, then, he can continue to assimilate experiences with his wife into his own favorable identity as a romantic husband, since he has no reason to doubt that his wife is happy.

Some comparisons of what husbands and wives in this group said about their marriage will illustrate this qualitative difference between partners in the salient features of spouse identity. For one husband, the most important problem that the couple faced was to maintain the relationship over time:

I think we both want a permanent marriage, and I think if you establish that as a goal, I think one recognizes that there is only one path to the means and that's harmony and that you have to make some concessions. . . .

In his wife's opinion, though their main problem was "the housework. . . . It's not religion, and it's not philosophy of life, it's not careers. Big items, I think, take care of themselves." This husband also believed he and his wife were romantically involved for five years longer than she recalled. Relative to his wife, he also provided an inflated estimate of the amount of time they spend together. When asked how much time he spends thinking about the relationship, he observed:

I think we spend a lot of time. I think this is reflected in our consulting each other, and the general acceptance that there's a more harmonious relationship when each person's feelings is involved in each decision that is being made. That is very important in our relationship.

When his wife thinks about the relationship, though, it is in: "thinking about something that we're about to do or are planning to do." Again, the wife focuses on the fact that a job needs to be done, while her husband is concerned with harmony and feelings.

Attachment to an idealized version of married life as a romantic escapade was another feature of their identities as spouses that appeared in the interviews of husbands high in intimacy potential. Thus, husbands would transform their perception of everyday activities in running a household so that they became expressions of their love for each other rather than the fulfillment of necessary duties. One husband described going to the grocery store as something he and his wife do together:

. . .because we get a kick out of it and set time aside for the two of us to do it together, it's time together. We do some planning before we get there and then do our meal and weekly planning at the same time.

His wife's version sounds much less enjoyable: "We just do it, when there's not a lot of food, one of us will go or we will go together." She is direct and matter of fact, and never mentions getting a "kick" out of what to her is an ordinary and not particularly pleasant feature of married life.

It follows that given their emphasis on romanticism in their identities as spouses, the husbands in these relationsips would focus more on the emotional than the practical outcomes of an end to the relationship. Indeed, husbands who described the emotional depths to which they would plunge if the relationship ended were invariably paired with wives who focused on what would happen to their finances, jobs, living situations, and ability to look after the children.

An opposite pattern of assimilation was observed among husbands married 10 years or less who had low intimacy potential. These men assimilated their experiences in the marriage through denial and assertion to arrive at as negative a view as possible of themselves as intimate partners. Compared to what their wives said, these men seemed to be unrealistically negative about themselves as spouses. The husbands were also more negative in their predictions of what their wives would say than the wives actually were.

This situation presents an interesting dilemma in terms of the rating of identity assimilation from self-report interviews. On the one hand, the husbands seem to have some stake in presenting their identities in as negative terms as they can. On the other hand, the wives are attempting to present their husbands more positively than would be warranted, at least on the basis of the intimacy scores of the husbands. Who is correct, then? The question is impossible to answer. However, it is obvious that assimilation is operating by both partners, and in different directions. The question of interest in terms of the identity-intimacy model is why husbands should try to present such an unfavorable view of themselves. This clearly contradicts the model of identity in relationships, which predicts that each member of the couple would be motivated to assimilate in the direction of enhancing their identities as spouses. In analyzing the responses of husbands in this group, an attempt will be made to arrive at an explanation of this unexpected phenomenon.

One of the least intimate husbands was convinced that his wife was perfectly miserable with him, and when asked how his partner feels about him, said: "I think she probably would have done better by marrying somebody else. I really don't know." His wife, to be sure, was not deliriously happy with their marriage, but she at least expressed much more optimism and acceptance of it than her husband implied. Similarly, a husband who felt that his relationship with his wife was heading in the wrong direction bolstered his negative identity as a spouse with numerous observations about just how bad their relationship really was. These observations came into direct conflict with those of his wife, who for her part was probably attempting to assimilate their experiences into her own favorable identity as a spouse. In the middle of the interview, the husband suddenly seemed to become aware of just how unfavorable his identity as a spouse was beginning to look. Perhaps he was conscious of some kind of reaction on the part of the interviewer to his answers, all of which were in an extremely negative direction up to that point. He then switched to the assimilation mode of justification:

All things being equal, we get along all right and it's funny, speaking to you and answering that questionnaire are two different things. If I read that now, if you read that and tried to correlate it with this tape, it wouldn't... everything is kind of medium to worse on that questionnaire, but when you sit down and compare it with what really happens, it doesn't come out that way, it comes out more on the positive side, but when you have to quantify it on paper and you are honest about it, can you honestly say you "almost never disagree with your husband," "almost never argue with your husband?" No, you probably have disagreements everyday. "Everyday" is down here with "every hour" and "never" is only up here. I'm saying to you life's not like that, but that's not what the questionnaire asks.... If you are honest it will look worse.

This was the only use of justification by husbands, it might be noted. It contrasts to the other-justification that wives used, which was directed toward protecting their identities as spouses by excusing the nonintimate behavior of their husbands.

In attempting to explain the identities of these husbands, whose existence had not been predicted, the answer must lie in part in the husband's identity as an individual, and in part in the dynamics of the marriage. It is likely that a man with a low potential for intimacy has for years been more introverted and incapable of expressing strong emotions, as the result perhaps of temperamental factors combined with the dynamics of his own early family experiences. This feature of his personality eventually becomes an integral component of his identity as an individual. He defines himself in terms of his inward orientation and discomfort with feelings, and preserves this self-definition as a means of maintaining a sense of continuity of the self over time. His wife's identity as a spouse leads her to try to see him as more communicative than he sees himself, but he resists accommodating to her attempts to draw him out because to do so would threaten his own sense of stability and the equilibrium their relationship has reached.

Accommodation

The most important change that husbands married 10 years or less believed they were undergoing as individuals through their marriage was change in their own personalities. It contrast to their wives, these men saw the main effect of the relationship to be one of furthering the growth of some quality within themselves. This development might have enhanced their identities as spouses, but its main importance to husbands was that it changed them in ways that generalized to outside the relationship. Wives were seen as the change agents in this process, but not because of any specific characteristics they possessed. It was the abstract concept of a "wife" that emerged as the dominant stimulus in bringing about changes in the identities of these husbands. The changes that wives described, it will be recalled, were very specific to the (perceived) features of the husband and the nature of their relationship. When wives accommodated, it was to the peculiar needs, interests, and personalities of their husbands. Changes in the identity of the wife as spouse were tied concretely to these qualities, as the wife attempted to mold herself to a form that would facilitate the relationship from her husband's point of view.

Husbands with high levels of intimacy thus described the identity changes they had undergone through marriage in terms of what the association with a wife had done for their personalities. When asked what would happen if their relationship ended, for example, this husband phrased his response in terms of the effect his relationship has had upon him. He noted that before they were married:

I spent an awful lot of time being somewhat self-destructive, I think. I really didn't have a very healthy attitude about things. I think that she's a real stabilizing infuence on me in a lot of ways and helps me to be a lot more positive and productive. I'm not so sure that without that kind of handle on things that I wouldn't just fly off and become real scattered. I think that it would be very negative.

The same kind of stabilizing influence was noted by another husband in this group:

I think I come from a background of very little responsibility. My past history as a boy, I think, reflects that and I think that's what brought me to my wife in that she is a very organized person, but over the past few years I've picked up some of those characteristics, because I knew they were assets that I needed.

This picture was verified by his wife, who observed that:

I think probably the cleanliness and orderliness of the house bothers me more, because I could see it coming even before we were married that this was going to be a problem. I would visit his apartment when he was a bachelor and I couldn't help straightening it out, because it wasn't like, I would have to clean the place up first before I would have felt really comfortable there. This is a problem a lot of men and women have because it goes back to their childhood to the way men were brought up and the way women were brought up and I think he likes the house orderly and clean, but it's not an obsession with him like it is with me.

Note too that in her description of her husband is a fair degree of "other-justification" of his untidiness. He developed his undesirable habits, she maintains, because of the way that he (and men in general) are brought up. The husband felt not only that he had gained in terms of his personal habits, but also in terms of his identity. If their relationship ended:

I'd feel like half of me was missing. I know I'm a dramatically changed person over the last so many years that we've been together and I've picked up new values, new interests, better ideas of responsibility, better planning of my life, time, budget, financial management. I've got some sense of organization which I never had before, so I would be much better off as an individual. I would have been the greater beneficiary of our marriage. If we weren't together anymore, I would probably be lost for a very long time.

What this husband valued in his marriage, then, is the effect of exposure to his wife on himself as an individual. One might almost say that the same outcome could have resulted from his acquiring a good business manager or vocational counselor. It is not so much his wife's particular characteristics that he valued but her role in shaping his personality.

When asked how he felt about his wife, another husband responded entirely in terms of how she boosted him when he was low and put up with his bad moods and idiosyncracies:

I need her around when things get tough or other parts of our life are really lousy, we want to be together. My free time, I can't imagine being without her, I can't think of anybody else I'd rather be with. I have other friends, there's nobody I'm more comfortable with. There's nobody that knows me better. There's nobody that puts up with my annoying little habits.

Clearly, this husband needs his wife not for herself as an individual but for her function in accepting him with all his "warts."

A similar process of a husband's incorporating the generic concept of a "wife" into his identity was apparent in an entirely different category of responses, those indicating a fundamental shift in one's identity from a self-definition as an individual to a self-definition as a member of a couple. One of the most highly intimate husbands described the relationship as:

...second nature to me now. Early on in my relationship...I guess everybody does...you think about your relationship a lot. I would think now I take my relationship with her in consideration when it's something that I think will impact on the both of us. It's so second nature to me now that I don't think there's any instance when I don't take it into consideration but I don't always have it in mind. It's a part of my consciousness, so any decision, I'm conscious of the impact it will have on my relationship.... I'm probably less of one person and more of two people right now than I ever was and ever will be.

Note that in this statement, he refers to the marriage as "my" relationship, a subtle indication of his accommodation not so much to his wife as an individual or an intimate partner but to the more abstract concept of being in a close relationship. Another husband's description of his feelings about his wife shares some of these features but with a different slant:

Although I rarely am sitting and thinking about my relationship with _____, my entire day is conducted in my brain almost as a narrative that is addressed to her. She's always with me in that respect.

It is not so much that thoughts about his wife as a person impact on his identity and change it in a specific way, but that his thoughts are addressed "to" her, for her to receive. This is another subtle nuance of language that reflects a one-way rather than an interactive process.

For these husbands, then, it is not the flesh-and-bood wife who permeates their thoughts, but the theoretical idea of a wife to whom their internal conversations are directed. Similarly, another husband described the root-lessness he would feel if he lost his wife. It was not so much that he would miss her personal qualities, but that he:

...would want to change everything entirely, I don't think to change identity but it would almost be that. I just wouldn't be the same person at all.

Perhaps this husband has some specific feature about his wife in mind when he implies that his identity has changed as a result of his marriage, but it is not evident in his response. Again, he is referring to the abstract idea of a wife rather than any particular features of her as an individual.

Given the high degree of intimacy that these husbands expressed in other portions of the interview, and in view of the romantic ideal to which they aspired in terms of their own identities, it is surprising to see the extent to which these husbands skipped over the particular qualities of their wives in describing personal change through marriage. After all, if they were so heavily taken with the idea of romance, would these men not be expected to be acutely sensitive to the whims and quirks of their wives and attempt to accommodate accordingly? The answer to this question might be "yes," from one point of view, but from another the answer is a clear negative, and for a good reason. These young men, with their romantic ideals about being a husband, are not as preoccupied with or aware of the more mundane features of their relationship. Their interest is far more heavily invested in their image of themselves as good husbands and their wives as agents of change in furthering this image. If their wife is not very intimate, the husband tries to draw her out in the best way he knows how, because that is what a lover is supposed to do. The particular issues on the wife's mind, which in many cases are the boring duties of everyday life, are not subjects that the husband necessarily wants to hear about, though. Therefore, we find women saying that their husbands are good "listeners," even when they do not offer specific advice, as this wife observed:

He's a receptive listener; he listens all the time, he offers an opinion when he feels it's necessary, he tries to help me, but in a lot of cases when I'm talking and I'm ranting and raving about something, I think he realizes that the best thing to do is just let me talk and I do. I talk and talk and talk and then I feel better. I get it all out.

The wife feels better because she has been encouraged by her highly intimate husband to open up and talk about what is on her mind, but there is no evidence that her husband is truly paying attention to what she says.

Husbands in this group gave other signs that, although they were high in the potential for intimacy, they had not truly bought into the model of "togetherness" into which their wives were trying to fit them. Even as close as they said they felt to their wives, these husbands referred to a need for independence and privacy or, as one husband called it, "a reserve of private thoughts that I don't share." Although these husbands assimilated their perception of their activities together into a romantic image, they still felt a need to define a psychological space between themselves and their wives. To one husband, then, their free time was spent almost entirely with his wife: "the two of us really have very little concern for what we do other than professionally as long as it's together." However, he also claims that each of them recognize that it is important to have separate interests (this is not what his wife says). As much as he says he needs and cares for her, he nevertheless shows signs of wanting more independence than he feels he has. At one point in their marriage, they fought over this:

The theme was I need your time, she was saying, and I was saying I can't give you any time, I feel overwhelmed, and so there were a lot of 4 A.M. conversations and a lot of discomfort because she felt isolated and kind of forlorn.

Now he sees them as "moving along in our own directions as well as together," a position not shared by his wife.

The need for independence may be seen as a further continuation of the ideal of the romantic spouse held by men with high potential for intimacy. To borrow a metaphor from fairy tale, Prince Charming does not spend his days and nights entirely in the embrace of his beloved. He also must pursue his own quests for fulfilling his heroic dreams. The romantically inclined husbands in this sample may not have been heroes, but they were aware of a need to develop as individuals outside the context of their relationships, as valued as those relationships were. Furthermore, it is likely that their "princesses" would become disenchanted with them if these men had no outside successes.

The husbands whose potential for intimacy was low gave responses similar in quality but less intense regarding their accommodation as individuals to the relationship. They did not speak of changes in identity or constant internal communications to their wives, but they did describe a feeling of comfort and security that their marriages had given them. The feelings of this husband toward his wife, for example, were that she is "a very valuable partner in helping me to understand myself." When he shares his worries and problems with her, it is:

...not because I am looking for a response but just to get it off my chest. Even if it starts out that way, she'll come up with some ideas and insights and we start talking some more.

The negative side of losing the relationship with his wife would be:

...to lose the home base. The perspective I need when I'm going through a job evaluation at work and I don't have any one else I feel I can talk to.

This man's wife serves a function in furthering his development as an individual and buffering him against stress.

Similarly, another husband regarded a good relationship as consisting of:

> ...being partners...I like to know when I have a problem confronting me that I have somebody here that I can sit down and talk to as an equal and get some intelligent feedback that's going to assist me.

As with the men whose potential for intimacy was high, these husbands described an accommodation process closely linked to their identities as individuals. It is not so much that a husband accommodates to the personal characteristics of his wife or the nature of their marriage, but that he develops greater self-confidence and self-understanding in the context of the relationship.

Changes in the identities of husbands occur not so much through the specific interactions they have with their wives, then, but through adaptation to the concept of "being married." Wives reinforce this process by placing fewer demands on their husbands to change in response to the wife's characteristics. This makes it unnecessary for the husbands to accommodate their identities to take into account the idiosyncratic qualities of their wives.

Couples Married Longer Than 10 Years

The main issue to emerge in the interviews of husbands in the longer-married couples was that of defining themselves as individuals with separate identities from those of their wives. The men with high intimacy potential appeared to be torn between wanting to see themselves as highly involved romantically with their wives versus needing to define themselves as free to pursue their independent interests and ideas. Men with low potential for intimacy were, in contrast, more "comfortable" with the idea of having integrated their wives into their identities as spouses. As with the younger husbands, these longer-married men did not refer at length specifically to their wives as individuals, but spoke of their wives in more general abstract terms.

Assimilation

The idea that their wives share their interests was a central feature of the identities of the more highly intimate husbands in the longer-married group. If the husbands married 10 years or less emphasized the romantic qualities of interactions with their wives, the husbands married longer than 10 years emphasized the extent to which their wives had come to take on the activities and concerns of their spouses. To a certain extent, this perception by husbands may have been an accurate one, based on our evidence that wives do in fact mold themselves to accommodate to the characteristics of their husbands. However, the husbands in this group seemed even so to be placing more weight on the degree of congruence between themselves and their wives than was warranted by the responses of the wives.

A husband whose hobbies were computers, sports cars, and stereo equipment, for example, insisted that his wife was just beginning to learn about these areas, and that her attitude toward his interests was that "she tolerates them with good grace." His wife's comment was, in contrast, less than gracious:

He loves his computers, he loves his cars, he loves his stereo. I can appreciate that he's very clever in these areas but they bore me stiff.

It is possible, of course, that this wife expresses her boredom "with good grace." However, her husband is apparently oblivious to her underlying sentiments.

Another wife expresses more direct resentment toward her husband's interest in his hobby: "I realize I am number two sometimes. The trailer gets a bath every week and I can't tell you the last time we had a bath together." He assimilates, though, his involvement in his hobby into his belief that "I think maybe I've gotten to the point where I've forgotten what I want to do and just concentrate on her." Although he admits that he is "maybe" more involved in the trailer than she is, he tries to portray himself as having sacrificed his interests to hers in the service of their relationship. This kind of assimilation is not so much an imposition of the husband's interests onto his perception of his wife's, but more of an attempt to see himself as a loving spouse who puts his wife above all else.

Longer-married husbands with high potential for intimacy also assimilated experiences in their relationships to a romantic ideal similar to that of the husbands married 10 years or less. One longer-married husband described himself and his wife as sharing many joint activities; included in his list of what they did as a couple was working "outside in the greenhouse together on weekends." His wife's account of this "shared" activity was much more prosaic:

Nominally, we'll work together, I mean he's at one end of the yard raking and I'm at the other end and we dump the trailer together. Or something really romantic like that.

His wife is aware that her husband is "a romantic," and in contrast to him, she focuses on the practical aspects of their relationship. If their marriage ended, she says, her reaction would be:

A. I'd sell this house fairly fast because I don't want to have to do repairs. In terms of my marital status I think I would prefer to stay single, and I think I would feel very comfortable.

Although she does not share her husband's identity as a spouse in a romantic marriage, she does seem to appreciate the fact that he tries to be egalitarian, and that he does emphasize the romantic. It is perhaps for these reasons that she thinks he would be "a hard person to replace."

In other couples, activities described in more separate terms by wives take on a decidedly romantic quality in the words of the husbands. This husband claims that what they do to be together is "activities mostly with our friends or just together as going out to the show or dancing or whatever." His wife's version of their time spent as a couple is considerably less idealistic: "If you can call together in the same room, he's watching TV and I'm reading." She makes no mention of the "dancing or whatever" referred to by her husband and indicates further that when they are together, they rarely share their activities.

The belief that he is part of an egalitarian marriage is another content theme of the assertion process shown by men with high potential for intimacy. One husband says that with regard to career: "I don't think I've ever made a career decision where she hasn't been a major piece of that." From her point of view, though:

It's mostly him with career decisions. . . . He will think things out a lot to himself, then when he has them all worked out in his head he'll present them to me.

The husband clearly sees his wife as more involved in his decision making than she sees herself. Again, it is not possible to determine who is "correct" here, but it does appear that the husband is distorting relative to his wife in a more egalitarian direction.

A somewhat clearer case of a husband's assimilating his behavior as a spouse to an egalitarian ideal comes from another couple. The husband claimed to discuss career issues with his wife, he says, because "she has the ability to project ahead, where I'm usually making quick decisions, so that's why I would discuss it with her." Apparently, though, his "quick decisions" are what remain salient to his wife, for she says he does not always discuss his career plans with her: "Two times he accepted a job offer that I didn't know about until he had accepted the offer."

This more behavioral data has the sound of greater validity but, of course, his wife does not mention how many times her husband did consult with her before accepting a job offer. Nevertheless, from the wife's point of view, anyway, her husband's behavior as a spouse does not conform to the egalitarian image he tries to present.

The identities that these husbands impose on their perceptions of their marriages share the romantic idealistic quality of the men married 10 years or less, but there are hints in the longer-married husbands of a greater emphasis on features of ideal marriages that the wives had as part of their own spouse identities. While the husbands selectively interpret the interests of their wives to match their own, they at the same time seem to have incorporated the views that their wives have of what constitutes a good marriage. Having made this accommodation, they then attempt to redefine their identities as spouses in ways that exaggerate the extent to which they meet these ideals.

Men whose intimacy was at a lower level assimilated their experiences with their wives to a "negative" identity as a spouse in the same way as had the men married under 10 years with low capacity for closeness. These longer-married men seem determined to prove to themselves and the world that they are incorrigible nonromantics who must be virtually impossible to live with and even harder to love. One husband, for instance, regarded the main problem in their relationship as the fact that he is not as "romantic" as he thinks his wife would like him to be. However, this issue is never raised by his wife, who claims that "if we disagree on something it's usually prioritizing what we need to spend money on." She apparently was not bothered by his lack of outward expression of feeling.

A husband with one of the most negative views of his identity as a spouse believed that his wife's reaction to the relationship's ending would be: "if she didn't say it would be wonderful not to have me around anymore, she is lying through her teeth." This is not, however, what she either said or implied anywhere in her interview. It appeared that she had adopted a realistic attitude of having come to a satisfactory resolution of an admittedly less-than-ideal situation and shown none of the extreme anger, even in disguised form, that her husband attributed to her.

Another husband expounded at length about how miserable he believed he was making his wife because of his difficulty in expressing feelings: "I'm sure that she would regard it as one of the great burdens that she faces in life, that I'm not a feely person." His image of himself in his wife's eyes also prevented him from sharing whatever worries and problems he might otherwise want to relate to her: "She finds it difficult to understand that a person who is extremely uncomfortable in expressing feelings could have a problem." It is as if he has set up an expectation in her now that he should not talk about his feelings with her, and so he has become trapped in his identity within the relationship as a nonintimate partner. In actuality, what he does not realize is that his wife appreciates the very feature about him which he fears she despises. If anything, she blames their problems on herself for being too emotionally reactive and "moody."

One of these husbands, in a series of responses to questions about his own intimacy, showed how damaging to the relationship the results of the assimilation process can be when it is allowed to operate unchecked by any accommodation to the partner's reality. The husband in his couple insisted that he could not tell his wife his problems because if he told her they would be signs of "weakness": "Why should I be leaning on her about that all the time if it's not something she wants to deal with?" The fact that he did not share his worries with his wife, of course, contributed further to their poor communication and lack of agreement on specific features of the marriage. Both of these factors would reduce the marital adjustment of the couple. The husband then went on to argue that he is less able than his wife to handle disagreements because he keeps things in too long:

I think I'm probably a lot more defensive than she is and in a lot of areas much more insecure and fearful. She's a much more aggressive person and appears to me to be a much more self-assured and much more confident person than myself.

His wife, however, believes that it is she who is unable to talk to her husband. Thus, his belief in his own ineptitude and his overestimation of his wife's personal resources prevented him from opening up channels of communication. Furthermore, this husband feels that he is "inadequate" to meet her needs for amusement and that he is unable to get along with her friends. In his wife's perception, though, "he is an easy 'get-together' person." Again, he seems to be assuming that he is a much less desirable spouse than his wife feels he is. Regarding their interests, which he sees as "worlds apart," he thinks hers are shallow and figures she thinks his, which are more intellectual, are a lot of "gibberish." According to his wife, though, these differences create no problem: "living 21 years with him I know what he likes and what I like. It's not bothering us too much."

The question, once again, is not whether he is right or she is right, or even whether his negative identity as a spouse masks hostile feelings toward his wife (a distinct possibility). The important issue here is that assimilation by the husband to a negative identity creates a twofold dilemma for the marital adjustment of the wife. First, these men have difficulty sharing their emotions with their wives, and this discourages their wives from being more intimate than they might otherwise be. Second, the assimilation that these husbands make to their inferior identity as spouses serves to set up artificial barriers to intimacy with their wives. The reasons for this will become more apparent when the accommodation used by these husbands is examined.

Accommodation

As much as the longer-married husbands with high intimacy potential pre-ferred to view themselves as romantically involved with their wives, they, more than their younger counterparts, showed signs that this is an area of conflict. On the one hand, they assimilate their perceptions of their marriages to their identities as spouses who are very closely linked to their mates. On the other hand, they describe changes in themselves through their marriages as involving movement toward a greater sense of indepen-dence as individuals. Thus, for instance, one of the more intimate men in this group noted that:

We've tended until recently to cultivate things together, I've modified my interests to be more congruous with hers and so has she. Recently we've started to say "well it's okay to pursue your own thing."

It is not clear that his wife shares this perception that separate activities are desirable, and it is not even clear that this husband really means it either. Throughout the rest of his interview, he talks at length about how close he and his wife have become and how important it is to maintain a high level of interaction between them. Indeed, it is he rather than his wife who periodically insists that the couple take some time to focus on their relationship and to get away from the distractions that cause them to lose touch. It is possible, then, that despite the implication of change in this response, this is an example of assimilation. The husband may be trying to maintain the image of himself as the romantic "independent" lover who can come and go as he pleases.

For another husband, though, the need for independence appears more authentic:

I don't think we're particularly fused in the sense that we have to have the same viewpoints. I guess we've got a lot of tolerance for the way that each of us does things or sometimes we even enjoy arguing about it.

Their separate interests are seen as an asset rather than a liability:

Well, maybe that's the basis of our relationship, sort of an attraction of opposites. I think that for a long time we tried to find, and we did eventually develop a common interest in the school committee. That wasn't even common to begin with. We weren't on the same levels that way either. And so that developed and we did find it strange for a long time because most people who were successfully married and were very attached to each other and did all kinds of things together and that didn't fit for us so we reconciled the fact that that just isn't the way things are going to be for us.

To his wife, this arrangement is a good one, but she still maintained that:

We're still kind of looking for something we'd both enjoy together. We haven't really found anything we're both just dying to get out and do together.

Indeed, the husband may not be quite as independent as he implies, as is evident in his observation that:

Our life at home to me is probably the most important thing in our lives, in my life. All the common, ordinary having breakfast together and that sort of thing, to me that is the more important thing in my life. Our life together is the reason we work and it's the most important part of my life.

What this and other husbands in this group are describing, it seems, is a very complex process of assimilation and accommodation around the issue of interdependence. The husband, to maintain a favorable spouse identity, accommodates to his wife's model of a "togetherness" type of relationship in which the couple shares every activity. However, in the process of making this accommodation, he becomes aware of compromising his own standards of being the idyllic romantic male who sets his own course of action. These standards may also be ones imposed on him partly by his wife, whose view of him is enhanced by his expression of independence. His only recourse is to attempt to pull out of the togetherness mode and develop his own interests and ideas. This is another kind of accommodation, one that is oriented toward developing his identity as an individual. There may be some assimilation involved, though, in the process of making this accommodation. The husband may fool himself into thinking that he is independent of his wife, but in reality he had become very attached both to her and to the model of relationship that she represents. He may also be playing out her scenario of his having outside pursuits that enhance his standing at home. It is this "hidden" kind of dependency that Rubin (1983) identified in her research, and it does seem to apply to this group of husbands. The difference is that the favorable spouse identity for this group of husbands includes the concept of being part of a "togetherness" marriage. They are more willing to talk about being dependent on their wives, even as they attempt to define themselves in more autonomous terms.

The situation of the husband with high intimacy potential, then, is very complicated and apparently very much in flux, with virtually simultaneous movement toward both assimilation and accommodation. Husbands with low intimacy potential accommodated in a much more straightforward manner. The changes they apparently have undergone over time in their perception of themselves as spouses are to see themselves as "settled" husbands who can relax in the context of a "comfortable" relationship. The relationship is comfortable, it may be hypothesized, because it does not present the same pressures for maintaining a high degree of closeness. The wives of these men have learned over time not to expect too much from them in the way of intimacy, leaving the husbands free to explore their needs of individuals without threatening their identities as spouses.

In the words of one husband, for instance, the relationship with his wife was "secure enough that I don't have to think about it a lot; I know it's there."

Another husband viewed his marriage as a:

...steadying factor...the way a rudder would be important on a ship...to the outsider looking at it might not look like it was that big a thing.

The relationship did not require much thought, said another husband, because "I guess we've become very natural to each other, I feel. So none of these things, I never think about them."

For men with low levels of intimacy, then, the relationship comes to be an accepted part of their identities requiring little thought or action. As such, it is appreciated but not unduly dwelt upon. These men, as they rest complacently on their identities as spouses, seem unaware of the extent to which their wives have grown away from them. The wives have accommodated to them by becoming less intimate in general or have found other outlets for their needs for interpersonal closeness.

Even the "negative identity" husbands show signs of accommodating to the domesticizing aspect of their relationship. One husband said that the relationship was a "steadying influence" and another that he would miss his wife if the relationship ended. In some ways, it might be even easier for these husbands to accommodate in this manner to the relationship because their wives would hold such low expectations that few demands would be placed on them and any signs of intimacy that they showed would be welcomed with relief and gratitude. The potential to maintain independence within a close relationship may be one of the reasons that husbands with low potential for intimacy develop these negative identities in the first place.

Ironically and surprisingly, it is the men with high intimacy potential who seem to have the most difficulty admitting to their dependency on their wives. In their efforts to meet the ideals both of the egalitarian mate and the romantic hero, these men are unsure of how to define themselves. It is also surprising that despite their high levels of intimacy, they manage to keep their ambivalence hidden from their wives. Men with low intimacy seem to have fewer conflicts around the issue of independence; perhaps by defining themselves as outside the range of their wives' efforts to reach them, they feel that their identities as individuals are on safer ground. In either case, it is clear that for husbands, issues of dependence and independence loom large in their identities as spouses.

4

Identity Processes in Couples

Having gained an understanding of the identity processes in wives and husbands as individuals, it is now possible to move on to consider the interaction of spouses in accommodating their identities to each other. The identity processes to be examined in this chapter include the mutual accommodation that partners make as they integrate experiences in the relationship into their individual identities as spouses.

Recall that to be considered as evidence for "mutual" accommodation, the responses of both spouses must contain reference to complementary changes undergone as a result of being part of the relationship. The statement by only one spouse was insufficient for this purpose, since it could be distorted in the direction of assimilation to that spouse's identity. The possibility remains nevertheless that both partners are assimilating their experiences in the same way to remain consistent with their individual spouse identities as both operate under the same illusion about their relationship. This possibility will be explored later in the chapter. At this point, however, the existence of concordance between partners in describing some specific aspect of their relationship can be considered a safe starting point for assuming that each has accommodated to a shared vision of reality within the relationship.

It is also important to remember, in reading through the comments by couples in this chapter, that the changes they describe are changes in their identities as spouses, that is, in their perceptions of themselves. There is no way of determining how much they actually have changed in their behavior as individuals or within the couple. What will become evident, though, is the extent to which their perceptions of themselves as spouses has developed in complementary fashion with the changes in the identities of their partners.

Although the analyses presented here are qualitative only, and thus no statistical comparisons could be made, it appears that the intimacy potential of the husband seems to have virtually no bearing on the outcome of mutual accommodation. This would represent a major difference from the findings concerning individual accommodation. It would appear, then, that regardless of the husband's capacity for intimacy, couples married over 10 years accommodate more smoothly to each other than couples married 10 years or less. In this cross-sectional study, it is of course impossible to determine whether it was this feature of their marriage that kept the longer-married couples together, or whether they had developed mutual accommodation as an adaptive means of enhancing their relationship. It is likely, though, that this type of reciprocal development of spouse identities is a process that evolved over time and is responsible for the endurance of these longer-term relationships.

A final methodological comment before proceeding to the interview material concerns the nature of the findings to be presented in this chapter. It can be assumed that when couples agree about some specific feature of their marriage, this probably came about as the result of accommodation. To this extent, agreement scores can be regarded as indices of mutual accommodation. However, without more details about the content of their responses, simple counts of agreement do not reveal the processes through which couples have arrived at this state of agreement. The material to be presented in this chapter richly embellishes the agreement counts with specific examples of how couples come to define themselves in complementary fashion. Although all the responses are based on self-report, it is still possible to detect the various lines of movement that the partners have traversed in their attempts to accommodate their identities to each other within the relationship. These analyses, then, have the most potential to exploit the unique nature of the data collected in this study, showing the exciting and dynamic interactive processes that can only be observed when both members of a couple are asked to respond independently to the same questions about their relationship.

Couples Married 10 Years or Less

Among the couples married 10 years or less, spouses were just as likely as not to arrive at complementary identities through mutual accommodation. When they did, they had come to reach agreement about some aspect of their relationship or had come up with ideas about how to improve their relationship. Some husbands and wives, for instance, described how through accommodation they had found better ways to resolve their problems. In one couple, the wife saw her husband's being "understanding, flexible, concerned about me" as having helped her to become better able to work through conflicts with him:

In the past I have tended to handle it by clamming up and just being a real bitch. And doing the silent treatment. I have really tried to get away from that.

For his part, her husband observed that when they have disagreements:

We try to deal with it immediately instead of storing it up. She tends to hang on to it. I can tell something's wrong. I tend to slink off into the corner and think about it. I've learned more recently to ask "Are you angry or are you just tired?"

Both partners, then, have accommodated to each other in this important aspect of their relationship. She is responding to his efforts to find out what is on her mind, and he is learning to come out of the "corner" and ask the right questions. This kind of mutual sensitivity is reflected in their views of what constitutes a good relationship: for him it is "compromise. . . and not worrying about winning and losing. . . a process." For her it is "acceptance."

For this couple, then, the accommodation process is seen by both partners clearly as having progressed in the same direction. The responses of the two spouses complement each other entirely. In other couples within this group, the accommodation process is seen as heading in two opposing directions. Both husband and wife in this next couple agreed that the wife is more reserved when it comes to sharing feelings. In her opinion, though, she has changed through his influence, at least in the area of settling conflicts:

He's helped me to do that more over the years. I'm just by nature more inclined to decide that I'm going to go away rather than talking it through and over the years I've become more inclined to talk.

This is not the change, however, that her husband perceives. The accommodation he has made is that "we've learned over the years to keep our mouth shut about that kind of thing." This may be one of those cases where the "truth" of what has actually taken place in this couple's relationship lies somewhere in between the "his" and "her" renditions of it. However, what is important is not so much who is correct, but the fact that husband and wife have arrived at such differing identities of themselves and each other as spouses.

The two examples were taken from the group of high-intimacy husbands. Similar patterns were observed among the husbands whose intimacy potential was low. Both members of this next couple, for example, had arrived at complete agreement about the nature of the husband's identity as a spouse. This was a negative identity, based on the husband's perception that he and his wife were miles away from reaching what he regarded as appropriate goals for their marriage. As he lamented: "Sometimes I say, God, things should be better, it's like I'm still waiting for everything to start." His wife, he claims "always says this is it, it doesn't get any better." Complementing this pessimistic analysis, his wife made the following observation about her husband:

He believes that if only "this" happened, everything would be perfect and long ago I realized that's what it is and so sometimes I think he thinks that if he didn't have a wife and a kid he'd do this and this not realizing that you only trade one set of aggravations and problems for others. . . .

Even though the accommodation this couple has arrived at is not one that particularly enhances their interaction, it does represent a shared reality. Just as common among this group, though, were instances of divergent outcomes of the mutual accommodation process. The husband in this couple, for example, believes that he has improved in his ability to settle conflicts with his wife:

Years ago it was hard for me to deal with it because she might say one thing and mean just the opposite. I couldn't read the signals and now I think through changes on both our parts—my ability to read her and her ability to say more directly what she wants I think that's becoming less of a problem.

From his wife's perspective, though, the accommodation has been far less than perfect. She believes that the way they handle disagreements is "leave me alone, back off." The husband is not completely unaware of the deficiencies that remain in their relationship. He thinks that problems they had in the past about him spending time doing things without her are getting resolved, that "even the way we discuss them is getting better." But he admits that this might not be completely so: "From another perspective, from inside them it seems like some things never get resolved."

There is some realization by this husband, then, that the accommodation they have arrived at is not a perfect one. However, it still remains clear that the couple's accommodation to each other has progressed along divergent trajectories. As if to reinforce this point, their observations about their different interests are also completely at odds. The husband's hobby, that he participates in without his wife, is hiking: "It fills a crucial need for me. . . . It's something that I don't have to answer to anybody else for." Because it "comes in conflict with her needs," though, he feels reluctant to devote time to this solo activity. From his wife's point of view, this is not the situation at all: "I encourage him and he encourages me a lot," she claims, in their outside interests.

Lack of integration of their identities as spouses seems fairly typical, then, of the couples married 10 years or less. The reasons for this may lie in the fact that the nonaccommodators have not yet ended what are destined to be failed relationships due to incompatibility, or perhaps because the spouses simply have not had enough time to adjust more fully to each other. In either case, they are at a point now in their relationships of having made less-than-ideal (and in some cases diametrically opposed) accommodations of their spouse identities to one another.

Couples Married Longer Than 10 Years

The predominant theme that emerges from the longer-married couples, particularly when they reflect upon what elements contribute to a good relationship, is that of mutual accommodation. One wife, for instance, described the advantages of this process as being that "you can be totally relaxed and honest and open, you can let that person see you looking ugly, you don't have to put up any fronts.''

Not only do they talk about adaptation to each other as important features of successful marriages, but many of these couples seem to have translated their ideas into actual practice. Their identities as spouses seem to have developed in complementary fashion such that they have adapted to each other's areas of strength and weakness, and they have learned ways of relating that allow them to maximize the chances of their getting along as amicably as possible.

The partners in one couple, for example, bend over backwards to avoid having the other partner worry unnecessarily. The husband protects his wife by not sharing his worries if he thinks it will upset her but encourages her to share hers with him: "I always tell her that if she shares a worry with me then she won't have to worry about it, because it's on my shoulders." His wife, though, is just as sensitive to overloading him with her own problems. She stated that although they are very close, there are some things she would not share with him because:

During this period of time when he's made the job change there have been some things that would have caused him some extra stress just in terms of some of the pressures that I was feeling at my job, but I felt that I could cope with them and I didn't need to bother him. So that sort of thing, recognizing his level of pressure and it's not that I don't care, he could know about those things, those would be things that I'd be sensitive to not overloading him.

Both spouses, then, see themselves as having to shield their partner from undue worry. In this regard, there is some assimilation in each of their responses. The husband thinks that he is being a good spouse in encouraging his wife to share her problems with him and by not telling her about his own concerns. The wife thinks, similarly, that she is able to read her husband's signs and meter out what she shares with him accordingly. The end result is that both spouses hold things back from their partners, but see this as consistent with their identities as spouses in a close relationship.

Mutual accommodation was also shown in the way that both partners in this couple had arrived at complementary views about the need for them to spend more time together. Both spouses were essentially in agreement on this point and, at the same time, gave evidence in their responses of having transcended the issue of whose fault it was that they did not spend more time together than they do. The husband observed that:

One or the other of us, it's usually me, in my perception at least, will take an opportunity to say "Wait, stop, things are going too fast, we're getting too sucked into our jobs. We haven't talked to each other this week. We've had one of those weeks where we've passed in the night. Let's stay home Friday night and just talk, or let's go to a movie, but let's shut the world out a bit, because we're losing the grip on this nucleus.''

From his perspective, then, this husband sees himself as the one who takes the initiative to see that the couple spends more time together. Analysis of the way he words this statement, though, reveals that he then shifts to the "we" form when attributing the cause of their drifting apart to both of them rather than solely to his wife. For her part, his wife admits to being the one that causes the couple to have less time together, and agrees that it is her husband who essentially brings her back into the relationship: "He reminds me that I'm putting in a lot of time at the office and fail to prioritize everybody else in the scheme of things." She thus takes total responsibility, and in the process protects her husband from the blame that he takes on by saying it is "we" who "haven't" talked to each other this week."

Given the attempts shown by these partners to exonerate the other from being the cause of problems, and given their sensitivity to each other's needs, it is no surprise that they define a good relationship as involving processes of mutual accommodation. The husband says that a good relationship means "Accommodation in the sense of thinking of the other person's priorities first, going that extra half of the distance." To her, it is "truly caring about someone to the point that you would give more than 50%. You would do anything you could for them." Both partners, then, have accommodated to the identity of a spouse in a good relationship who countributes more than half to the total quality of the interaction. Obviously, both partners cannot technically give more than 50%. The perception that each has done so enhances both of their identities. This perception probably also enhances their ability to maintain a high quality of intimacy in the relationship.

Mutual accommodation can also result in both partners agreeing that it is one and not the other spouse who is to blame for various defects in the quality of the relationship. In one couple, for instance, both partners concurred that in a disagreement, the wife is the one who tries to talk things over and the husband is the one who pulls away. They also agreed that they differ in their styles of communicating with each other; that it is he, not she, who is inept at self-expression. His spouse identity, then, is of a negative kind (although not as extremely negative as other husbands) and it is maintained through interactions with his wife that continue to validate this identity. The wife's spouse identity is that she is the one who attempts to engage her noncommunicative husband in the relationship. In reality, though, there is a large discrepancy between these results of the accommodation process and the way the couple behaves. This husband and wife had high scores on the communication task, indicating that both were in fact very well able to express themselves to each other. Furthermore, in contrast to the identity that the partners had worked out for the husband, he appeared to be quite willing to expose his feelings within the relationship, as his intimacy potential was high. The data from this couple illustrate that the result of the mutual accommodation process need not correspond to the identities the partners formulate for themselves.

Although the concept of partners accommodating to each other might have the connotation that the process leads to greater mutual understanding and closeness, this is not necessarily the case. Couples may accommodate to the idea that there is something very wrong with their relationship, as in the case of a couple who both recognized that they had begun to grow apart. According to the wife, "If seems to me like we talked about more important things before we got married than after we got married." Her husband also indicated, although more obliquely, that something significant is lacking from their relationship:

It's so easy to get caught up in spending the time doing other things...we have to schedule time to spend with each other and if you don't do that, it's easy for the relationship to deteriorate.

Although he did not come forward and state their marriage is deteriorating, his statement is compatible with that of his wife. Both partners, then, see flaws in their identities as spouses, and thus are both accommodating to the reality that there are competing demands on their time that have interfered with the quality of their interactions.

The mutual accommodation a couple makes may also involve movement away from each other on the basis of interactions in which their areas of disagreement have become so painfully obvious that they can no longer be discussed. They may decide, as one couple did, that they have to make decisions independently of each other to avoid getting into arguments. The husband in this couple felt that he and his wife have to get:

...better at creatively dealing with our expectations of one another, and giving the other person space to make their decisions. And for me, not thinking that every decision that she makes is like a decision that I have to live with. She can make her decision and we can go off in a certain direction and I don't have to feel like it's my identity that's being lost.

This man was one who had high intimacy and expressed in this statement the need, also expressed by others like him, to be more independent within the relationship. The difference between him and most of the other husbands with high intimacy potential was that his wife was very poorly adjusted in the marriage. She too expressed a desire to gain more independence from her husband, whose aggressive penny-pinching had become a source of great annoyance to her. If their relationship ended, she predicted that:

Well, I would probably feel a certain degree of freedom in the sense that I would, just financially, I would do things maybe a little differently. That I think would be a little different...I would do some things unique to myself that wouldn't be influenced by him at all 'cause he has such strong feelings on everything. His identity is so strong that I sometimes have to say, you have to know when your identity has to just stay with you and not pull me into it. And some ways I want to find out what am I without that shadow there.

Who initiated this process of mutual accommodation is, of course, impossible to determine. However, given that wives tend more to accommodate to the identities of their husbands than vice versa, one hypothesis is that the husband was the first to perceive the need to define a separate self. His wife, sensing his movement away from her, then moved in an equal but opposite direction on her own separate track.

Mutual accommodation can also take the form of couples moving away from each other due more to a benign kind of neglect rather than as the result of an active decision-making process. The spouse identity is so taken for granted that the individual believes it requires no work to keep it alive. This may be seen as a negative development in a way, in that it has the potential to lead to the death of the relationship through atrophy. On the other hand, it may also be seen as a favorable development in that when couples reach this point, they have become so much a part of each other's identity that they experience a comfortable sense of security within the relationship. The comments of one couple on this point capture both the pros and cons of this type of accommodation. When asked about the relationship enduring, the husband begins by describing his reaction to the questionnaire, in which one item concerns whether the resondent "desperately" wants the relationship to continue:

It's something that was a funny question on that thing. I...."do I desperately." I don't "desperately" want anything. The next one "I want very much." I guess I never thought about it, because it's never been threatened. The way it was phrased was as though the relationship had been threatened. So none of those questions pertain to the situation I'm in.

He does not think much about the relationship, he said:

Lying in bed at night, I don't think am I doing everything correctly. I guess we've become very natural to each other, I feel. So none of these things, I never think about them.

His wife, though not so explicit, indicates that she herself has gone through a similar process, and that she does not think much about the relationship either: "No, not with so many other things happening that we really don't spend a lot of time thinking about it." For this couple, then, there is not an excess of conscious thought devoted to their spouse identities, because these identities form so much a part of their underlying sense of self.

Among couples characterized by serious problems in communication, limited capacity for intimacy, and differences in personal styles and outlooks, mutual accommodation processes take the form of emphasizing the need for "compromise" if a marriage is to remain intact. One husband with low intimacy potential observes that compromise is important to a good relationship and that, with respect to arguments, "I think we've matured to the point that we think it's not worth it." To this, his wife added that:

Just a few years ago we realized that we were really good friends and we have a lot of time and we're very comfortable with each other. It's a long-term investment. There are really no problems that we don't handle on a day-to-day basis...you have to learn to put up with someone, what you don't like about them.

Their joint efforts over the years to resolve their differences through this maturation process have led, in the wife's estimate, to an improvement from "25 to 99%" in the quality of their relationship.

The importance of mutual accommodation was apparent even to one of the most poorly adjusted longer-married couples. Both partners in this relationship had low intimacy potential, and both were at the bottom of the distribution on marital adjustment scores. Yet, both husband and wife regarded accommodation as the crucial feature that kept their marriage intact, despite its many problems. From the wife's point of view, "You have to compromise...if it's not a terrible kind of a disaster, you should stay together." As bad as the husband believes their relationship to be, he is convinced that mutual accommodation has worked in their favor:

Over a period of time, I think both of us have learned how not to do that as far as dwelling on negative things and being personally hurt by petty things a lot less now, say in the last 5 years than in the first 15....

Both partners, despite the serious differences that they both believe exist in their backgrounds, regard mutual respect as a feature of a good relationship. And despite the many disagreements they have and their divergence of opinion on many basic issues, he felt that:

I'm probably much closer to my wife, or she is to me than either one of us realize, whether it's just bonding that takes place over time or what have you....

His wife also acknowledges feeling closer to him than to anyone else, again, despite what she admits are fundamental differences in personalities and outlooks.

Another couple whose adjustment was better but who still described major differences in personal style and communication had developed mutual accommodation as a survival strategy. As the husband observed:

We just don't expect to agree on things and consequently don't tend to develop the kind of minor-league bickering that I've seen among other couples.

The relationship has endured, he said:

Because we have had on a number of occasions to make adjustments to changing circumstances, to accommodate changes that we've wanted and we've always done that.

His wife, who is higher in intimacy than he, seems to be somewhat more open to accommodating to his needs and interests. Nevertheless, the process of accommodation is clearly one that has taken place on both sides of this relationship. She says that working in harmony is important, and "the more we pursue things and grow as a person the better it gets." Perhaps she is operating under somewhat of an illusion in that her husband regards their differences in interests and personalities as having enhanced their relationship. However, she seems to be addressing a similar theme as he, that their relationship has improved the more they have been able to compromise through mutual accommodation.

Couples also accommodate by learning each other's styles of communicating and adjusting their ways of relating accordingly. A husband whose own potential for intimacy was low noted that:

She normally can tell when something's wrong and I can tell when something's wrong with her and we pick at each other and find out what it is.

Not everything is quite so rosy, though. He claimed that he does not argue: "That drives her up a wall, that's my way of getting back at her."

His wife admits that in these situations, she gets upset and starts hollering and "He sometimes walks away from me, but that makes me madder." Both agree, then, about the nonproductive way in which they argue, and even if it is not a particularly good way to achieve resolution of their differences, the fact that they give the same story suggests that their spouse identities have developed in parallel regarding the kind of relationship they have. Similar to other couples in this group, the two partners refer to the process of compromise. The husband defines a good relationship as "a process of give and take," and the wife observed that:

We've both matured enough to sustain each other. I think we came a long ways, because we've had a lot of disagreements over the years. I'm surprised I stayed as long as I did with him. We've had some bad years too.

Through what was probably a very unpleasant time for both of them of arriving at compromises in their identities as spouses, this couple has managed to achieve a reasonable state of equilibrium. There still are the annoyances involved in their method of handling disagreements, but these are the product of the same kind of mutual accommodation process of learning about each other that has allowed the couple to be able to sustain each other within the relationship.

Another way the mutual accommomation process can work to ensure the harmony of the relationship is to help the spouses learn how to avoid habitual sources of conflict. In one couple, this took the form of not engaging in any kind of competition because, as the husband observed:

Both of us are quite competitive and any kind of competition or game it's very difficult for me to compete with her. I don't want to beat her, but I hate to get beaten so we tend to avoid that.

This is the opposite situation of the previous couple, who had learned, over the years, exactly how to get under each other's skin.

It was the longer-married couples, then, who showed most clearly the kind of growth as individuals and as couples that characterizes the process of mutual accommodation. It is this process that allows couples to gain, if not a more realistic picture of the relationship over time, then at least one that their partner shares. The common understanding that both spouses have can then be used either to enhance or to sabotage the relationship. For the relationship to endure, however, the ratio of these two outcomes must eventually be tipped in the direction of improving the couple's methods of communication and conflict resolution. When this happens, even relationships characterized by misunderstanding and petty differences can be perceived as satisfactory by both spouses.

Relationship Between Mutual Accommodation and Communication Scores

From what couples say about the accommodation they have both undergone through their relationship, it would appear that a great deal of identity change has taken place in each partner. However, this analysis of self-report material cannot answer the question of whether mutual accommodation has really changed the spouse identities of the two partners. Do the identities of partners actually develop in complementary ways or do the partners develop complementary perceptions of their identities? For practical purposes, the question is moot, since what is important in terms of how the couple gets along is that they believe themselves to have compatible identities. From a theoretical perspective, however, the distinction is an important one. According to the identity-intimacy model, experiences within the relationship should have the potential to mold each person's identity through the accommodation process. An alternate prediction is that the two individuals in the relationship form their own reality to which they are both accommodating their identities. This reality does not correspond to the couple's actual experiences, but it is a shared perception of what the couple has endured together. It is this perception that will influence their further development as individuals and as a couple, not their objective experiences. Over time, the shared reality held by the partners becomes more and more similar as they each accommodate their identities as individuals to it. Presumably, even if this shared reality is light years away from the couple's objective experiences, accommodation to it can be an adaptive process for the couple. The danger is that if the discrepancy between the perception of reality and its objective features becomes too great, the couple will be unable to adapt to the world outside their relationship. The most extreme case of this is a *folie a deux*, in which the couple shares a psychotic view of themselves and others. They both agree completely with each other, but the agreement they have reached differs radically from the reality of the outside world's. In a less bizarre instance, a couple who has an identity of themselves as happy and harmonious might find themselves shocked to be excluded from their bridge club for being too argumentative whenever they play a losing hand.

A very simple analysis was possible with the present set of interviews comparing the extent to which the couple's mutually agreed upon views about the relationship were corroborated by the scores the couple received on the communication task. It might be expected that couples who had accommodated to each other in such a way that they agreed more or had adapted to each other's identities should have higher communication scores than those who had not. Conversely, if the accommodation reached by these couples was an illusory one, then there should be no relationship between the objective index of communication and the couple's joint statements about how well they had learned to understand each other. As it turned out, couples who provided testimony to the high quality of their mutual accommodation to each other received scores no higher on the communication task than couples who did not consider themselves to have reached a shared perspective on their relationship. The divergence between the quality of the couple's communication and their perception of the relationship was greater in the longer-married couples. Of the nine couples who showed signs of using mutual accommodation but whose communication scores were low, eight were in this group. Of the seven couples with high communication who said they had accommodated to each other, four were married less than 10 years.

These results are based on very small numbers but do correspond with the observation that longer-married couples make of the complacency associated with their perceived state of mutual accommodation. These couples seem to have gotten the idea that in a relationship characterized by high understanding and good communication, it is not necessary to talk. When both partners make this assumption, though, the understanding that they achieve of each other is likely to deviate more and more over time from the reality of their situation. Limitations in their ability to relate to each other do creep in as they stop talking. We will explore this question more fully in Chapter 7, when we examine the way the couples performed on the communication task.

5
Identity Processes in Power Dynamics

The distribution of control within the relationship is a potent area for conflict between spouses. Each individual is likely to have his or her own ideas about who has more influence, and these ideas may or may not be in agreement. According to the identity-intimacy model, the spouse identities of the two partners include ideas about the power distribution within the relationship, both the perception of it as it really is and the ideals of how the spouses think that power should be distributed. The model also is based on the premise that the identities of the spouses, rather than some objective quality of their relationship, is what will influence their interactions when it comes to issues of control.

There was a strong tendency within this sample for the traditional power attributions to be made of control over sexuality to the husband and over domestic affairs to the wife. As can be seen from Table 7 in Appendix D, wives were more likely to have power attributed to them in the area of practical concerns; husbands were seen more in control in the sexual aspects of the relationship. Sex as a specific area within the identity-intimacy model will be discussed in Chapter 6.

The distribution of responses to questions about practical matters according to husband-wife agreement, shown in full in Table 8 of Appendix D, suggests some further complications in the processes of power attribution within this domain. When wives and husbands agreed that the wife was more in control it was, most frequently, on the question of who made the decisions about minor, everyday matters. Wives readily admitted to having greater control in this area, and their husbands absorbed without difficulty the awareness of the greater influence held by their wives. When wives and husbands disagreed on the question of who had greater power, wives were over two times as likely as husbands to see themselves as being the dominant partner. The greatest discrepancy between husbands and wives occurred on the question of whose wishes take precedence in the practical area of the relationship. One possible reason for the disparity on this question is that wives who have the greater responsibility for minor decisions generalize from this to the assumption that their power extends to more important concerns as well. Husbands, in contrast, make a clearer distinction between the minor decisions and the heavier concerns that arise in the practical realm. This situation creates a dilemma for both partners when it comes to reconciling their identities as spouses with their experiences regarding the practical aspects of their relationship. We shall look first at the problems that arise for the wives.

Assimilation Processes in Wives

Wives who believe that their wishes take precedence over those of their husbands are presented with a conflict between their experiences in the minor decision-making aspects of the relationship and their identities as spouses in egalitarian relationships. They have been led into thinking that they hold greater power in the relationship by virtue of the fact that they make many of the minor household decisions. At the same time, though, their view of themselves as holding the greater share of power conflicts with what their husbands believe. This conflict creates difficulty for wives who attempt to adapt their spouse identities to fit with the way their husbands view the relationship. Furthermore, we have already seen that wives attempt to adapt their spouse identities to be consistent with the view that they are partners in egalitarian relationships. The idea that there is a disparity in decision making does not fit with this view. The upshot of these conflicting perceptions is that the wife adheres to the view that she does play a major decision-making role, while at the same time discounting the importance of her power or excusing it in some way.

A relatively clear-cut example of this process comes from one wife married 10 years or less who, while admitting that she plans more of their activities than does her husband, adds that she "likes to think" that she consults with her husband. Her meaning can probably be taken quite literally here, because she presumably does "like to" think that her husband has an equal share of power. That this is most likely a distortion is corroborated by her husband's response that it was his wife who did more of the planning. A more complex example comes from another couple, in which the wife's response indicates her conflict over the question of who plans more of the couple's activities:

Sometime during the week we say, do you want to go to a dinner or a play, or I look at what's going on and say "These are our options, what would you like to do?" It's usually up to me to get the baby sitter and make all those kind of arrangements. Only if there's a couple of choices, then we usually talk about what we'll do or who haven't we seen in a while that we ought to get together with and make some choices about that.

The interviewer, to clarify the double message conveyed in this response, asked further:

But in some cases you know you're going to be going out so you might go ahead and make the arrangements without consulting him too much?

The wife's response to this was, "Yeah, lots of times." This would suggest that indeed, the wife does make more of the decisions and that her earlier response represented her attempt to cover this up as much as possible, both from herself and from the interviewer. Furthermore, the transition from use of the pronoun "we" to "I" in her first response is so subtle and yet so automatic that it suggests that she frequently uses this strategy. As it turns out, her husband has become convinced that the process is in fact an equal one, as is evident in his response:

We usually look things up to do in the paper, we'll hear about things from friends and we just talk about it, do we think it will be fun and we discuss it and we say okay, that's what we'll do this weekend.

The wife had, then, apparently managed to translate her spouse identity as an equal partner in the practical area so convincingly into her behavior that her husband was unaware of her making arrangements without his knowledge or input.

The wife in this example did not resist assuming power, but did resist admitting it. The case of another couple shows more clearly the way that wives resist assuming the dominant position within this area of the relationship. The husband responded that he consults with his wife on practical aspects of their marriage, but believes that his wife would prefer that he make decisions independently of her. The wife asserts that no one person makes more decisions. It is possible that the husband's perception is inaccurate, but it is more likely that it is the wife who transforms her perceptions so that they fit with the ideal of egalitarianism consistent with her spouse identity.

The tactics used by other wives to transform their perception of their own dominance into a model compatible with their identities as egalitarian partners took several more specific forms than this example, adding interesting new twists onto what has already been observed in the prior analyses of identity processes.

Other-Justification

Many wives resolved the conflict between their spouse identities and their perceptions of having greater power through the other-justification process. The most direct examples of this involved the wife's stating that her husband did not have control in this particular area because he was too busy, not a well-organized person, or had some other similar limitation. Rather than take the awareness of this limitation as a sign of their husband's inadequacy, though, these wives managed to transform it into a virtue. At the same time, they downgraded their own superior organizational or planning skills.

The wife cited in this excerpt gave the following justification for her husband's lack of control or involvement in decision making:

I guess it seems like I probably have more free time, possibly that's the largest controlling factor of who makes the decisions, because he is working and in school both, and presently I just have work. I have a lot of extracurricular activities outside of work, but I don't have such a rigid schedule like he does, my schedule is more flexible, since I can probably pick and choose the activities I have outside of work, I can limit them if I choose to, whereas he has work and school, that's a given thing.

Her greater "free time," then, is what provides her with the opportunity to put extra time (and influence) into the family decisions. However, as she points out, she does have a lot of "extracurricular activities" so her free time is really not so free as she originally implies. It is the extra time that she has, though, that gives her the justification for having her wishes take precedence over those of her husband:

I might be a little more dominant there to see that my wishes are fulfilled, because I feel like I put more into it, the planning, so maybe I just streamline it so.

If she justifies her dominance as due to her putting in extra time, then this takes away from the stigma of being the controlling partner in this aspect of the relationship. Even so, she is not able to accept this justification without ambivalence, and she goes on to refer to herself in a derogatory fashion as being more "selfish" than her husband because she streamlines the planning so that it turns out in her favor. Later in the interview, however, she admits that perhaps some of the reason for her greater influence in the practical domain is due to the fact that she is "a little bit better organized," an observation shared by her husband, who notes that "I think she's more organized in the development process of our family relationship and activities." This seems like an "approved" area of expertise, then, for the wife, and she is aware that her husband knows she is better organized than he. In this couple, the husband agrees that the wife has her wishes acceded to more often than he does, but it is because "she has spent more time thinking things out than I have." This further reinforces the wife's perception that her control rests on her having greater time, not greater influence or even competence in this aspect of their relationship.

The admission that she is in control, even in the traditionally "feminine" realm of the marriage, is not an easy one for these wives to make, as indicated in this statement by a wife when asked how the situation came about:

I hate to say it, but stereotypical female...I think some of the things I feel that I have a little more expertise about, about the children, doctor's appointments, day-to-day things like the kids, clothes, food.

This is something the wife does "hate to say," because it violates her spouse identity, as indicated further in her elaboration of this response:

I guess even though sometimes I begrudge that I make all those kinds of decisions, I guess it's because of the role that I have assumed. . .not always willingly, but I do it.

This wife does not refer to her husband's attitudes toward her dominance in the practical area, but the responses of other wives do support the idea that it is necessary for the wife to perceive that her husband does in fact want her to be more in control in this area of the relationship. In almost all of these instances, though, the husbands perceive the situation to be one of equality. Therefore, it would seem to be the case that the wives in these situations have performed a double kind of assimilation. They first take greater control in the relationship but then use justification to assimilate this perception into their identities as egalitarian spouses. They accomplish this assimilation by seeking attributions other than a desire for dominance as the cause of their greater influence. At the same time, they justify their greater control as consistent with what their husbands want anyway, and in the process even manage to make it appear as though their power were an unwanted burden. As one wife says, "I make most of the decisions, I think, as far as the house is concerned because he doesn't like to be bothered."

Other wives maintain that they are home more, that they are good at household organization or that their husbands are too "busy." From the standpoint of their husbands, though, it is not so clear that the wife is sacrificing her own interests to meet the needs of the household. One wife did admit that:

I run things. I think it's by mutual accord. He would take care of the house and typically I do the housework. It's not that he can't but I don't like how he does it. And it's an equitable division of chores because that's how it works not out of any oppression of one or the other or traditional. It's just that I'm not good at some things and he's not good at others.

Her husband's interpretation reflected less favorably on her and their situation. According to him, he does not help her when she is busy "because my wife is the type of person that you can never do anything to her satisfaction." Although his wife did admit to not liking how he does the housework, the "mutual accord" she refers to probably came about through a different process than she implies.

A more nearly parallel set of accounts comes from another couple, who both agree that the wife makes more household decisions because she is more efficient and that if she waited for him to make a decision, no decisions would get made. She maintains, however, that he at least has a veto power: "If he doesn't like it, he would tell me, but most of the time yes, he goes along with them." Her husband is aware that his wife "allocates to me in her mind a veto power." He insists, though, that he does not use it and that: "I really do kind of like it, I may complain, but I probably trust her decision making." He is aware of her impatience with his inability to make a decision:

I'm sure if you talk to her she would say "Well, if I left the decision making up to him in that area, we wouldn't ever do anything, we'd never move off a dime because he doesn't want to do this or he wouldn't want to do that, or he'd be too frightened to do something else," and I think I recognize that and felt it would be better to let her make decisions because then things would get done.

A new wrinkle is added, though, when he acknowledges that: "if there are mistakes then I can blame her for them. I don't have to take responsibility myself."

What happens in effect is that the husband "grants" to his wife the power to make major decisions. He has not communicated this to her directly, but has through his actions shown that he is not going to be pressed into service. Furthermore, by allowing his wife to take responsibility, he manages to achieve the added benefit of being able to criticize her when things do not go well. This couple was, as may be apparent, one of the less-well-adjusted ones in the sample. The husband was very low in his own potential for intimacy, and although very willing to open up in the interview, seemed to have major axes to grind about his wife's behavior in the marriage. His passive aggressiveness toward her, as exemplified in his responses, was hidden behind his veneer of being, as she described, "an easygoing person."

A similar complaint was lodged by another husband, whose observation contrasts sharply with his wife's optimistic appraisal of the power dynamics of their relationship: "Sometimes I'm the boss and sometimes he is and I don't ever get the feeling that there's a vying for power of dominance." But from her husband's point of view:

She always says you make the decision...it's like I made the decision but in reality we both made the decision. Because if I say "No" I hear another two hours of conversation of why we bought this television versus the one I wanted to buy at K-Mart.

Apart from the fact that the couple does not agree about whether they alternate or whether she "always" tells her husband to make the decision, it is apparent that the husband feels that whatever decisions he makes are contingent on his wife's approval. However, later in the interview she does admit that: "To be really blunt, I think it's a really equal division; he makes the money and all the rest I do." With this statement, she does acknowledge that the power in the relationship rests with her after all. Perhaps her assimilation of the relationship into her spouse identity was not as total as among the other wives. Indeed, considering that she was in the group of wives married 10 years or less, she had lower marital adjustment than wives whose use of assimilation was more pronounced.

Another way that wives use other-justification to assimilate their experience of having greater power to their identities as egalitarian spouses is to redefine power so that their husbands appear to share an equal role in decision making. This wife illustrates such a process, commenting that who assumes more responsibility for everyday decisions "depends": "I usually do the cooking, about 95% of the time, so I decide, but he does the dishes, so he'll decide when to wash them." The decision of when to wash the dishes seems hardly equivalent to the decision about what to cook, but by allocating to her husband this "responsibility," the wife can maintain her belief that she and her husband share equally in this aspect of their relationship.

Another wife and her husband both agreed that she makes more everyday decisions than her husband. According to the wife, though, she has been allocating more decisions to him recently: "Yet I've been giving him the responsibility of which child is going to watch which cable program they wish to watch." The children's television habits may be an important consideration in this household, but it again appears to be only a relatively minor area of everyday decision making. Her husband seems, despite his wife's efforts to give him more responsibility, to have trepidations about asserting himself. He said that he helps her when she is busy and tries to:

Think ahead or don't ask her, I'll just go ahead and do it which may a lot of times work to my disadvantage because I may catch hell for it because I may move something.

Before making a decision, he needs to check with her because "if I don't ask her advice, it won't get done the right way, it will get messed up." For this wife, then, it is apparent that her husband has not adjusted to her redefinition of power as much as she might think.

The redefinition of control is also apparent in another wife's observation that when it comes to practical aspects of the relationship "I would do it for both of us, equalize." What is immediately apparent in this statement is the paradox that if she does it "for both of us," how can it be equal? It would appear that the wife is trying to maintain an identity of herself in an egalitarian relationship even as she admits to the disparities between this identity and her experiences in the relationship.

The redefinition of power used by other wives takes the form of the wife assuming that the decisions she makes are in the "best interests" of her partner. In this way, she can claim the greater share of decision-making responsibility, but redefine it as an expression of her husband's "real" needs. In the words of one wife, she makes the decisions about practical things "without a whole lot of debate about it. . . and I know the things that he doesn't agree on."

In another couple, both partners agreed that it is the wife who makes everyday decisions, but as far as whose preferences are followed, the husband believes the power balance is equal. The wife believes that perhaps her wishes are followed "a little more"; that "he'll give in to me but it's really what he wants to do." By assuming her husband's wishes are the same as her own, she can reconcile the conflict between her spouse identity and the perception of her experiences within the relationship.

Wives use other-justification, then, to assimilate their perception of their husband's lack of power into their spouse identities as egalitarian partners. They also attempt to redefine "power" so that the role of their husbands in decision making is reinforced.

Denial

This form of assimilation appeared in the responses of wives who claimed that their husbands made practical decisions or that the control was shared jointly when, in contrast, the husband asserted that the decision-making power was held by the wife. A straightforward instance of the wife's denial of power comes from this couple married 10 years or less, in which the husband replies that regarding major family decisions "I think she has a little bit more of an edge. I think she's running around 55%.... She's usually right by the way." For her part, his wife maintained the opposite position:

I would say that his wishes probably take precedence over mine because that's the kind of person I am.... I'm a person that gives in more than other people anyway, unless it really rakes me wrong.

Clearly, this woman's identity in the relationship, and perhaps outside as well, is as someone who concedes to the wishes of others. When it comes to paying the bills, her husband maintains that "I don't really have to know, and she does a good job." His wife, though, claims that they discuss "everything" involved in household decision making. The power that her husband is attributing to her is not something that she is willing to accept.

Another couple echoes this disparity, with the wife insisting that she and her husband "share responsibility" for major family decisions and the husband holding the view that she makes more of these decisions: "She's a stronger character than I am." More explicit rejection of power comes from one of the wives in the longer-married couple group. Her husband attributes 60% of the decision-making power to her, and she evaluates their power distribution as more nearly equal. If she were to have more power "it would make me feel very uncomfortable. I would never do that." Later, she acknowledged that "maybe in terms of upkeep of the house I do, but both of us just hate that whole thing." That "whole thing" means a power differential, which this wife does not want to acknowledge. She then goes on to upgrade her estimate of his contribution around the house: "I have the feeling that if something were to happen and he were no longer here, the house would not be quite as organized."

Resistance to admitting her greater power is a tendency seen in another of the wives married over 10 years, whose husband described her as:

Somewhat more highly opinioned on some matters than I and consequent to that her wishes are more forcefully expressed on occasion. She feels very strongly that such should be done on a particular occasion that it's definitely time that a certain piece of furniture be replaced. I'm less inclined to be as emphatic.

His wife, though, feels that:

Things are about equal, occasionally mine are because I come up with new ideas of things to try but for the most part they're equal.

Although she ventures to admit that she might have greater control, this wife immediately downgrades the importance of this. Furthermore, she denies having greater say than her husband on everyday matters, power that her husband readily attributed to her.

The conflict between her husband's attribution to her of power and her own unwillingness to admit to it comes through in the response of another wife in the longer-married group, who observed that:

We have been discussing the fact that I've got three kids and they think Daddy's the boss and when you ask Daddy he says Mommy is. I felt really bad about that.

What this wife apparently felt bad about was that she was given this power by her husband. She consoled herself with the thought that:

He allows me this power. If he thought it was important enough to fight over it then he would. He doesn't think it's important enough to get upset over. He allows it, so therefore I have assumed control. I would say my wishes and yet we have a furnace sitting downstairs that I didn't want. So.

The idea that her husband "allows" her the power is one that emerges in the responses of husbands when they justify the fact that their wives have greater authority in the practical aspects of their marriage. For this wife, the resolution that it allowed her reduced potential conflict between her spouse identity and her experiences in the relationship.

A wife in the longer-married group who averted the dominant role in the practical domain gave as her reason exactly this kind of unwillingness to accept authority. Both she and her husband confirmed this in their complementary responses. He said that he plans their recreation and leisure because "she gets nervous over making plans for the two of us, just in case, she has never enjoyed it." He does not specify what the "just in case" refers to, but his wife did in her response. She gave as the reason for her husband taking on greater decision-making authority the fact that "I have a tendency to think that if I choose something and he doesn't like it I feel guilty." The way that she does take on somewhat greater power, though, is through an indirect method of becoming the better organizer. The husband noted that:

Sometimes she's into making lists and boards and charts for the kids so I don't think she discusses it with me too much if she does that for the kids.

The wife's assertion that they do discuss these practical matters can, in this light, be viewed as an attempt to deny the power she has covertly assumed.

For wives, then, acknowledgment of power outside the limited range of minor everyday decisions presents a major threat to their spouse identities as partners in egalitarian relationships. They either attempt to bolster the role of their husbands in the marriage or deny their share of responsibility. Husbands can also be seen to use assimilation to protect and preserve their own identities, often toward the same goal.

Assimilation Processes Used by Husbands

The assimilation used by husbands is focused toward fitting their perceptions of the power distribution within the marriage to their identities as romantic males. They prefer to view the relationship as a loving, close, and companionate one, yet they also have an image of themselves as somewhat autonomous within the union. Their ideas about power, then, emphasize equality and when inequality is perceived, they need to find a way to excuse their lack of control. Thus, they develop views about the dominance patterns within the relationship that complement those of their wives. They either justify their situation or deny it, by refusing to recognize their wife's power in the practical domain.

An extreme example of assimilation can be observed in this couple in which both partners admitted that the dominant partner in the relationship is the husband. It is somewhat incongruous, then, that both partners agree that it is the husband who concedes during an argument. As the wife said:

He tells me that he's more apt to give in if there's a fight...probably 80% of the time he would give in and then we would end up talking about it and getting it settled.

Notice here, her response is phrased as "he tells me," showing that she feels she can admit to having greater power because it has been cleared with her husband. In any case, her account is consistent with the husband's, who says that he does "give in" when they fight, and that "I feel that when I do apologize we can joke about it and then we can...talk about it." This comment was prefaced by the observation that "it's not that she's right or I'm wrong...." He has allowed himself to save face, then, by sidestepping the issue of who is to blame. The spouse identity of this husband, shared by both partners, is therefore not threatened by the discrepancy between it and their experiences within the relationship.

A converse situation existed in other couples in which the husband maintained control over the relationship but allowed himself to maintain his identity as a romantic mate with the paradoxical assertion that he "lets" his wife have more influence. This husband said that:

In the past I asserted myself a lot more than she had, but recently she has started to assert herself more and more as she's had more authority. A good example of that is she's insisted she's going to have a piano for Christmas.... I think she's going to get it.

Nevertheless, he says that he retains control over major investments but that "the wife" makes more decisions about the budget. The reason he asserted himself more in the past was that money was tight, but now that they are earning more, "I let up a lot of control and especially household expenditures." Does the wife really have more power, then, or not? She seems to think that they do "come to a consensus" on most expenditures. However, by virtue of his "letting" her have more influence, it would appear that he still holds the reins. Framing the situation in these terms allows him to retain his identity as an egalitarian spouse and gives the wife little ground on which to challenge hers.

Self-Justification

Other more straightforward instances of husbands assimilating their spouse identities onto their experiences in the practical domain fall in the category of self-justification. One husband using this mode of assimilation claimed that:

Major family decisions I think I probably have the most influence over, though I think the ideas are presented by my wife most. . . . I think she puts a lot of weight, though, on my approval or disapproval of the idea.

His wife, however, believes that it is she who makes major family decisions. In the husband's response, though, it is apparent that he is attempting to resign himself to the possibility that his wife has the ultimate authority in this domain.

Other husbands preserve their spouse identities by finding covert routes around the areas controlled by their wives. It was generally not possible to evaluate the responses that fell into this category in terms of assimilation because the husbands were reporting mainly on "successful" routes to avoiding the notice of their wives. For example, a husband in the shorter-married group had found that:

She is more willing to let me have more say in my outside activities and hobbies if she knows that those activities will not stand between her and myself.

From his response, it appears that he has to receive his wife's "permission" to explore his own independent interests. This places him in the somewhat restricted position, nevertheless, of having to find activities that interest him and yet meet his wife's demands. By claiming to engage in this process voluntarily, he manages to remove the onus of not appearing egalitarian while at the same time giving himself the option of developing his autonomy outside the relationship.

For one of the other husbands married 10 years or less, a similar maneuver allowed him to accept simultaneously his wife's greater power in the financial area along with his identity as a spouse in an equal relationship:

She pays most of the bills. . . . I don't take it on with active interest, but I know what's going on. She thinks I don't know what's going on, but I know what's going on.

His wife, at the same time, presumably has her own identity conflicts reduced by her husband's apparent willingness to concede to her wishes in the financial domain.

By admitting to having less power than their wives, but claiming to have found a way around their wives' area of control, these husbands manage to feel equal and independent even though, by their own admission, it is their wives who dominate in the practical area of their marriages.

There were a few couples in which the husband insisted that he deferred to the majority of the wife's wishes. One husband in the longer-married group reflected on his marriage in these terms:

We always discuss things but I was always interested in making her happy and whether she feels we need a new living room furniture or rug or whatever. Whatever made her happy I felt was the thing to do. I don't have any particular strong feelings. . . . We discuss things but in a certain way I don't have very many things to contend in those areas. When it comes to children for some reason I always wanted to have a couple more than we have. She didn't feel that we could emotionally handle more and now she feels we can't emotionally handle kids. I've deferred an awful lot of things to her. Whatever she's most comfortable with. . . I'm very happy living with her. I think she has a very narrow spectrum of what she would like her husband to be like and I think that was part of the reason why we decided to get married or she decided to marry me. Because I fit into a very narrow category of exactly what she wanted. On the other hand, I think I probably could have married a couple of different types of girls and lived quite comfortably.

There is a hint of self-justification in this response, in that the husband sounds as though he is just a shade too easygoing and adaptable to be real. As it turns out, on the basis of other responses he made, the situation is not quite a clear-cut as he implied. In talking about how he presents criticism to her and how the couple resolves disagreements, he described the process as follows:

I think we both have a very aggressive, abrupt background. We feel perfectly free telling each other to go jump off a bridge or argue or fight. . . . We holler and scream and, we don't wreck the house or hurt anybody physically, but. . . . .

The things they argue about are, he continued, that:

I think we tend to be too perfectionistic so we have to knock each other down once in a while in those respects when you get too anxious and carried away with what you're doing. And a lot of times, there was a time when the kids were very afraid to see me get angry and I knew they were and now I can blow off steam and make a joke about it. And we can fight and joke our way through just about anything.

His wife never mentions the aggressive style that her husband insists they "both" have. It seems quite likely that the husband in this relationship has a spouse identity as a soft-hearted, flexible husband, but that his behavior probably has a more tyrannical element to it. The fact that his hobby is playing ice hockey suggests further that this man is not as gentle as he likes to portray himself within the context of the relationship.

Husbands also assimilate decision-making experiences within the relationship by justifying actions that they take unilaterally as being in the "best interests" of their wives. One husband in the shorter-married group expressed this tendency as follows:

She has had a problem knowing exactly what she wants. Therefore, in that kind of vacuum my wishes might take precedence, because I might know and she might go along with them.

He has apparently succeeded in convincing his wife that her wishes are followed, because she observes, "I think sometimes my wishes may tend to determine what we do." Oddly enugh, she believes that the main problem in their relationship is for her husband to feel "more in control of his life." This husband, then, had convinced both himself and his wife that by making a decision in his wife's best interests, he was doing nothing more than serving her. He had done such a convincing job of this, that his wife believed he lacked control over his own life decisions.

Other husbands assimilated the power distribution within the marriage to their spouse identities as equal partners by ignoring or minimizing the attempts of their wives to accede to their husbands. The analysis made by one of the husbands married less than 10 years of the decision-making process in his marriage reads as follows:

Major decisions of all types, we try to talk as much as possible, but at the point of an impasse where we seemed to have talked so much about it and there still is no clear answer, but we still have to decide, we just decide one way or the other and I wouldn't want to say either one of us either takes the initiative to make the final decision more than the other.

This answer implies that there is a joint, mutual process of arriving at major family decisions. It contrasts sharply with his wife's account of this process:

A lot of times we'll sit down and talk and I consider him a lot wiser than I am and a lot of times I'll defer to him, but only after we've talked about it because I feel that I have an opinion and I should voice it, but he makes a lot of the decisions. It's not as though I feel that that's wrong. A lot of times I am very supportive of his decisions and we finally have talked it out and gotten down to that.

This response represents a complex mixture of assimilation to two competing spouse identities. On the one hand, the wife sees herself as deferring against her will to her husband, but on the other hand, she regards him to be the wiser one and so lets him decide on the outcome of their discussion. Her husband, though, is apparently oblivious to his wife's efforts to accede to his views or else decides not to mention this observation in the interview. In either case, his response is a gesture aimed at assimilating his greater power into an egalitarian spouse identity. In another response to the question of helping her spouse when he is busy, the deferential aspect of the wife's identity is more strongly displayed:

I try to keep quiet and not talk if I can. I busy myself. I have needlework. I sew, I knit, I do all kinds of quiet things that I do, or clean. I save a lot of my cleaning things until night after we finish watching TV. At night, he gets to work and I get going on my things. I just have to be as quiet as I can because the apartment is small and he's real busy and he needs a lot of concentration and it's hard for him if I'm not real quiet.

She also sees herself as receding into the background in the area of career decisions:

He's worked so long and so hard that I think when he gets to the point where he's got to make a decision, it's up to him to decide what's best for him without worrying about me. When he went to graduate school, it was real hard because I had to say I wanted to come to Buffalo so badly because my family is near here. . . . It was real hard because I wanted to say "let's go to Buffalo," and I couldn't. I had to let him decide what was best for him because he's worked so hard for it and I think that's what's going to happen at the end of the year when it's time for him to start picking jobs. He has to pick the job that's best for him.

His perception, though, is that career decision making is an equal proposition and he says "Oh, yes," to the interviewer's question about whether "the kinds of things she would say to you influence any kinds of career decisions that you might make." Thus, in the husband's mind, the relationship is a partnership of equals, and this is consistent with his spouse identity. His wife's observations, which are compatible with her identity as a deferential spouse, have little correspondence with the husband's. A similar denial of power was seen in another of the couples married over 10 years, in which both partners agreed that minor decisions were made mostly by the wife. When it came to major decisions, though, the situation became more complicated. The husband said that his wife made more of the household decisions because she is at home more than he is, but that "really big" decisions were made through joint discussion. His wife's account throws this analysis into a different light: "I kid him about that. He lets me take care of the little things and if it's a major thing he has to give the OK before it's done." To "give the OK" is not exactly the same as discussing, and the wife's response implies that the husband is attempting to downplay his role in the decision-making process. This possibility is further reinforced by the wife's comment that:

I'm not sure whether that's really true or not, but I have a sense in the back of my mind that if he got a job that took us across the country we'd all pack up and go, but if I got a job like that there would be a lot of foot dragging.

This husband prefers to see himself as an egalitarian partner, then, but in his actual behavior communicates to his wife the message that he would rather not accede to demands made by her.

Overall, there seems little difference in the assimilation processes used by husbands and wives in the area of reconciling disparities between a spouse identity as an equal partner and the perception of inequities in the power balance. Both husbands and wives wish to avoid seeing themselves as having the greater share of decision-making responsibility. The explanations offered by husbands and wives do seem to differ, however. The dominant wife finds it necessary to excuse her greater power and justify her husband's failure to assume a more prominent role as due, perhaps, to her having more time than he has. The dominant husband makes no such effort. The weaker wife accepts more readily her husband's dominance over her; in contrast, the weaker husband seeks a justification that parallels that of his wife.

Accommodation Processes

The adaptation of one's identity to that of the partner's or to the "reality" of the experiences within the couple constitutes accommodation by the individual. Examples of this process came, in the present sample, from wives but not husbands. One of the reasons that wives rather than husbands used accommodation is that wives tended to have more power attributed to them anyway, and so felt secure enough to examine any possible challenges to their position. As stated by one wife:

If I know he really wants to do something I'll do it because he so rarely is that strong about something. He doesn't ever dominate me, so that if I can sense that he really wants to do it, we'll do it. But it's not because he forces me, I really love this guy and I want to give back. The only reason he would have any more say than me is because I would let it be that way.

This wife seems comfortable enough with the power balance in the relationship that she is willing to give over some of her decision-making power to accede to his wishes. It is important to remember in this context that the wives generally preferred to see their husbands as having more power. Therefore, they may have been hypersensitive to even minor indications of their husband's wishes and preferences. Another wife, in the longer-married group, described the way that she adapted to her husband's nonverbal signals. Implicit in her response is the idea that she is willing to concede because he grants her enough power to allow her to feel secure. Regarding leisure, she claimed that:

We find out what the other one would want to do. I don't know always if he really wants to do it or if he is just going along with me. We consult with each other. I'm probably more outspoken if I really don't want to do it, but I've learned to read what is a neutral look in him is negativity.

For a wife in a much unhappier situation, accommodation has meant learning to anticipate what will aggravate her husband and responding accordingly to keep peace:

I generally know what he'd be upset about, like if I don't get a generic product, that's important to him. Like on milk. I personally would like to get a gallon of regular milk. He grew up with powdered milk and I've gone with this because I'm not a regular milk drinker. Now he's started demanding generic powdered milk and I bristle at this because I think milk is important to the children. . . . So I reacted by getting regular liquid milk. I know this sounds crazy, . . . so then we talked about this again and we decided we'd stop playing this game and we'll go back to getting the store brand.

Her feelings about having won this small battle (but still having lost the war) have not eased her general resentment over his maintaining strict control over the couple's finances. She talks very candidly about how she has reacted to her husband's attitude toward money:

In the money realm, although he doesn't even have to say anything to me. . . I can already hear it or I'll put words into his mouth and then I get angry, before I've even talked about it. I would say that I perceive him to have a greater control over money than perhaps he even does, because I generally do get what I want. It's just every single little purchase, I'm conscious of this, it feels to me that he has a greater control over me in this than I wish he did. . . .

This response indicates accommodation in two ways. One, she admits to the existence of flaws in the relationship such that her spouse identity as a wife in a close and happy relationship is challenged. The second feature of accommodation illustrated in her response is her description of how her perception of her husband has invaded her daily conscious thoughts.

Other instances of accommodation, these from some of the wives married 10 years or less, show similar attempts to take a relatively objective look at their situations. Such an effort can be seen in the following interchange between the interviewer and the respondent:

Wife: I'd say that one's wishes take precedence, but if I'm being real honest they're split equal. Sometimes I get into the "poor me" syndrome, but honestly speaking. . . .

Interviewer: Sometimes it feels like your husband.

Wife: Oh sure, all the time.

Interviewer: But when you sit down and take a look at it things are pretty equal.

Wife: Yes, when I'm being totally honest and rational about the whole deal, we're pretty much equal.

It is possible that the wife's response at the end of this interchange represents assimilation of her "poor me" experiences into her identity as a spouse in an egalitarian marriage. However, with the statement that she is being "honest" and "rational," she certainly gives the impression that it is in her moments of feeling dominated that she is using assimilation. One will never know the "truth," of course, but what can be seen in this response is an attempt, at least, by the wife to take a different perspective on her view of herself in the relationship, and this attempt would seem to qualify as accommodation.

In another couple married 10 years or less, comparison between the answers of husband and wife suggests the use of accommodation on the wife's part. The husband claims that on major family decisions, "We talk it over all the time. We talk most things over." His wife responds that she makes these decisions, but then adds:

He probably said he did. I think I probably do. He probably goes along with what I want more than I go along with what he wants, but somehow it ends up being usually what we both want. I think if it's a toss-up, it usually goes my way.

This is a rather complicated statement, and if it is dissected, it reveals several facets of the wife's identity processes. It is evident that she uses accommodation in evaluating her husband in that she is able to give a relatively close prediction of his response. Furthermore, she admits to having more power, and whether or not she is correct, this differs from the efforts of other wives to view themselves as equal partners in the practical area of the relationship. With her assertion that what the couple "ends up" with is what both of them want, she verges on assimilation (seeing what her husband wants as consistent with her own desires). However, the way she phrases her response ("it ends up being usually what we both want") does suggest a process of compromise that causes the end product of their negotiations to be acceptable to both of them.

With this response, we begin to move into the area of mutual accommodation. This process involves, minimally, statements about the importance of compromise in the marriage and, at best, evidence that both partners have moved their positions as a result of exposure to the other. Instances of mutual accommodation were found primarily in the longer-married group, and this is a finding consistent with those reported in the separate chapters on husbands and wives.

Some couples make explicit the importance of mutual accommodation, as in one couple who agree that no one's wishes take precedence because both are willing to compromise. In other cases, one or both partners talk about equity having been reached over the years as each partner takes turns in having his or her wishes met. As one wife observed:

I can think of specific examples where my wishes have been followed, but on the other hand where his have too, so it probably goes down the middle, but I think we take choices and try to assume responsibility for what we do, sort of share.

Both partners in this relationship had agreed that no one's wishes took precedence over the other's. A description of this process was echoed in another couple, who agreed on many aspects of their relationship but gave slightly different responses to the question of whose wishes take precedence. According to the husband, they each compromise. His wife observes that:

I guess it's about equal. It's hard to know. I usually get my way. It's usually equal, usually it's not very different so it doesn't seem like there's a lot of compromise.

Perhaps what happens in these couples is that after many years of mutual accommodation, it really is "hard to know" which wishes are whose.

In another couple, the process of compromise seemed to take place in a staggered fashion. Both agreed that no one's wishes took precedence. According to the husband, they are both "pretty agreeable," and in his wife's view he is the one who is open and flexible. Furthermore, she sees this as an ideal toward which she strives. This process appears to be accommodation within accommodation, then, with the wife trying to change herself within the context of a relationship in which both partners accommodate to each other.

What these couples illustrate, then, is that the distribution of power within the practical area of the relationship can proceed in a smooth fashion despite differences in spouse identities and partners' expectations of what characterizes a good relationship. With each partner willing to make concessions to the other, each one's identity as an egalitarian spouse is actually reinforced, more so than if each were simply assimilating their experiences to their ideal versions of what constitutes a good spouse.

6
The Role of Sexuality

The area of sexuality brings together many of the most sensitive issues that spouses face in terms of their own identities and in terms of the way they view their partners. In no other area of marriage is one's spouse identity more vulnerable and interactions more open to misinterpretation. This is particularly true for the cohort of couples studied here who are too old to have been exposed to sexually "liberated" attitudes in their own growth and development. However, exposed as they are to the current media presentations of the idealized views of adult sexuality as unreserved and unihibited, the people in these couples face many possible challenges to their views of themselves as sexual partners. These couples are also old enough to have retained ideas about male dominance in sexual relationships, ideas that were reflected in the attributions of power by both husbands and wives regarding who has more control over sexual interactions (see Chapter 5).

All of these influences present numerous opportunities for the kind of identity assimilation process that distort a spouse's perception of self and partner. At the same time, however, the importance of sexuality to the total quality of the marital interaction would tend to motivate couples to resolve their misunderstandings through identity accommodation. In this chapter, we shall look at both identity processes as they apply to the area of sexual relationships within the marriage.

There were few differences between the couples married 10 years or less and the longer-married couples with regard to their reliance on identity processes. Whether assimilation or accommodation was more frequently observed in the younger or older group was not as apparent as in other areas of intimacy. There were, however, striking gender-related themes in the content of the assimilation and accommodation processes. The spouse identities of husbands and wives diverged sharply in some areas of sexual intimacy, in ways that seem highly related to very traditional stereotypical views of masculinity and femininity. We shall examine these gender differences within the framework of the identity processes.

Assimilation Processes

The forms of assimilation evident in other areas of the relationship, including denial and self- or other-justification, were also evident in the area of sexuality. One new form was, however, observed only in the sexuality part of the intimacy interview. This form emerged, in part, for structural reasons due to the nature of the questions. Compared to other areas of the interview, there were more questions in the sexual area in which spouses were asked to predict the response of their partners. The form of assimilation that became evident in the responses to these questions was for the spouse to claim lack of knowledge of the partner's position on a particular issue or question. A simple "I don't know" or "I've never talked it over with her" was the typical responses representing this form of assimilation. It is possible to speculate that the reason the "don't know" form of assimilation became apparent in the sexuality questions is because of the nature of the topic. In this, more than in other areas of the marriage, it seems likely that couples would be inhibited by embarrassment from communicating some of their deeper fears and reservations, as well as their preferences. As one husband in the younger-married group observed, he does not like to talk about sex because "there isn't much to talk about, you do it."

The reason that "I don't know" is considered a form of assimilation is that the spouse taking this position is claiming to be unaware of the reality being experienced by the partner. If this is a true lack of awareness, it means that the spouse is out of contact with the partner's feelings. If lack of knowledge stems from a more defensive stance toward not knowing the partner's difficulties or complaints, it is even more clear that assimilation is at work. This was apparent in one couple whose relationship was extremely conflictual in most areas, but particularly in the area of sexuality. The husband observed that they do not talk about sex "because, again, there are life philosophies and things involved there and we have a wall between each other." The wife, in turn, claims that she does not know if sex is important to her husband or not, and neither seems to know if the other is satisfied. The husband says their relationship is "unremarkable," and assumes that she is dissatisfied; she claims their relationship is "routine," and does not know how he feels. Whether the lack of knowledge about each other is due to indifference or the kind of "wall" to which the husband refers, it is clear that the inability of these spouses to integrate the experience of their partners is a major obstacle to mutual facilitation of their spouse identities through their interactions with each other.

A couple might also attempt to find out where they both stand with regard to a particular aspect of their sexual relationship but be impeded from coming to a mutual understanding of each other due to the complexity of the issue. As one wife in the longer-married group stated: "We've discussed some of this, but it's hard to know where somebody else is." This wife seems to have made an attempt to accommodate to her husband's experience, but was unable to, perhaps because his messages were not always clear. She stated that she is not sure if he can refuse her sexual advances:

I tease him about having headaches once in a while, but I don't think he does. I mean I don't think he refuses me, not that he doesn't have headaches, he could.

What appears to be assimilation on the part of the spouse, then, may actually represent the partner's unwillingness to let himself be accommodated.

The "don't know" form of assimilation was observed in couples where one or both spouses claimed lack of knowledge of the partner's position. Husbands and wives seemed equally likely to use this form of assimilation. For instance, in one couple, the wife claimed lack of knowledge about how her husband feels about refusing her sexual advances. He stated the following in response to this question:

It's easy to refuse because most of the times when there's been a refusal it's a situation where the spirit is willing and the flesh is weak because it's late at night.

The wife is not sure how he feels about this topic, because she has not "checked it out with him." In another couple, it is the husband who claims not to know his wife's position on a question. She says that she does hold back sexual interest when she has uncomfortable feelings about her husband, and that her husband does not: "Does any man?" When they stop, she adds, is up to him "being a male." Her husband responds that if she does hold back sexual interest he does not know about it. In this couple, the wife's stereotyping of her husband as a typical male is obviously fairly extreme. However, apart from that, it is clear that her husband has chosen not to attend to this negative feature of their sexual relationship.

In general, an individual who is attempting to maintain a favorable identity as a spouse in a well-functioning marriage will deny problems and obscure the negative features of the sexual relationship while at the same time asserting that the relationship is sexually very free and easy. The husband in one couple, for example, believed that he was physically expressive, as was his wife. His wife, maintaining that this does in fact hold true for her, observed that her husband is expressive only "when things are going well"; that otherwise "he becomes very introverted." Another husband in the shorter-married group asserted that it is easy to ask for sex and easy to refuse, and that his wife thinks so too: "We've got a happy marriage, everything's easy." His wife, however, says that it is in fact difficult for her to refuse his sexual overtures, and furthermore that it is difficult for him too; "it rarely happens." This husband's assertion of how good their sexual relationship is contrasts strikingly with his wife's observation. He never holds back sexual interest due to uncomfortable feelings, he said:

Because sexual activity is the result of good feelings, I would say that is never a question. It's an automatic thing when we are harmonious together that there's no deliberate hold backs. That's because our feelings are in sync.

His wife never holds back either, he claims. According to his wife, however, both of them do hold back. Either the wife is being unduly pessimistic, which would be assimilation to a negative spouse identity, or the husband is exaggerating the extent to which they are "in sync." The fact that he is not aware of his wife's perception of the relationship, though, would tend to mitigate against the validity of his claim.

As even more obvious case of a husband's tendency to deny the negative and assert the positive came from another couple married 10 years or less. The wife observed that because the couple is trying to start a family, their sexual relationship has become "regimented." According to her husband, though, "it's usually an automatic thing. We don't have to work on the calendar for spontaneity." It is of course possible that the wife is trying to become pregnant without her husband's knowledge, but it is more likely that the husband is minimizing the constraints put upon their sexual relationship by the need to follow the biological timetable.

Wives also showed this kind of assimilation, in which they "missed" seeing the disappointments or unhappiness expressed by their partners. In one couple, for example, the husband admitted that it is difficult for him to refuse his wife's sexual advances. His wife reported that he had no problem refusing her, but that was because he rarely did: "To tell you the truth, but it would only be like if he'd been on a motorcycle trip for two hours and was dead, you know." On the one hand, his infrequent refusals might signify that he indeed had difficulty saying "no" to his wife. However, his wife clearly implied that for her husband, refusal or participation is a straightforward matter. The wife is not simply imposing her own view onto the situation, but is blocking out awareness of her husband's own doubts and concerns about himself. Another husband, for instance, insisted that his wife does not hold back her sexual feelings because of uncomfortable feelings toward him. His wife, however, stated in a very matter-of-fact way, "Usually if we have had a fight or argument, it's very difficult for me to think about being intimate." Thus, the wife admits to a problem that she has which her husband either is impervious to or has chosen to ignore. Another husband similarly believes that he has no problem refusing his wife's sexual invitations, and that neither does she. Her response, though, indicates a considerable amount of ambivalence about the matter:

That's tough, I suppose that's tough for all women. Who knows what's on your mind? Maybe you're tired or maybe you're thinking it's just going to be the same damn thing.

Not only does she acknowledge difficulties in refusing her husband, but she also expresses considerable dissatisfaction with the couple's sexual interaction in general.

There is a subtle distinction between this form of denial and the general denial of problems in the relationship. A spouse's denial of problems in the relationship includes denial of his or her own difficulties. The denial of problems expressed by the partner implies that the spouse is unwilling to admit to unhappiness that the partner alone is experiencing. It is possible that the partner in this case has not communicated his or her unhappiness to the spouse and that there is no way that the spouse could have guessed that the partner was having difficulty. However, in this case, one must ask what is preventing the partner from bringing to the spouse's attention these particular problems. One plausible explanation is that the partner is not anxious to interfere with the spouse's more optimistic view of the partner's adjustment.

Related to this "other-denial," as it might be called, is another form of assimilation in which the spouses present their partners as being "better" sexual partners than would be indicated on the basis of what their partners actually said about themselves. Spouses who used this kind of assimilation seemed intent on believing that their partners regard sexuality as important and are sexually proficient. This occurred, for example, in one of the longer-married couples regarding the question of the husband's sexual preferences. The wife stated that her husband had no such preferences. When asked whether his wife knew about his preferences, however, the husband asserted that she did and that she "sometimes" accommodated them. Along the same lines, his wife expressed her belief that sex is more important to her husband than to her. Assimilating her lack of enthusiasm to his spouse identity, he gave the following rationalization for his wife's apparent lack of interest: "The actual sex is more important to me but that it be a satisfying relationship for both of us is equally important to both of us." Part of this husband's spouse identity, then, involves seeing himself as married to a partner who finds sex to be an important part of the relationship.

Along these lines, a prominent theme in the responses of the wives married 10 years or less was that sexuality was more important to their husbands than to themselves. The wives insisted on holding this position, even though it conflicted with some of their own observational data, as in the following wife's response. This wife stated that sex is more important to her husband even though she is the one who initiates it more. Realizing this discrepancy, she stated: "I think I just contradicted myself, but I think it is more important to him." Her awareness of the conflict between her spouse identity and the data from her experience does not prevent her from arriving at a conclusion that apparently reflects an assimilation process.

Another wife's response, compared to that of her husband, seems to reflect a similar process. Her husband provides a finely differentiated analysis of the couple's relative degree of sexual interest. The wife, he believes, "wishes we had it more often." Preoccupation with his work interferes, he claims, with his "getting in the mood." Recently, however, his wife seems to be less interested herself, "so it's kind of like in theory she would like it more often but in practice it doesn't seem to be that way." In view of this observation, the wife's response that sex "might be more important to him" seems to reflect the process of assimilating her perceptions of her husband into her spouse identity as being less interested in sex than he.

Altering the definition of "important" is the route used by another wife to bolster her perception that her husband values the sexual aspect of their relationship. Both the husband and the wife in this couple agree that the wife is more interested in sex. The husband's perception is that sex is more important to his wife. His wife maintains the view that sex is "equally important" to both of them with the qualification that "the way we approach it is different."

The perception that she has diminished her own sexual interest was observed in another wife within the shorter-married group, who believed that sex had become less important to the couple over the years. As she observed:

In the beginning of our marriage it was very, very important to me because it was more validating each other's attraction to the other, but as we have grown together it has become less important.

From her husband's point of view, however, sex remains more important to his wife than to himself. This situation presents some intriguing possibilities from the standpoint of identity processes. The wife may be using assimilation in her perception that her sexual appetites have waned as a means of preserving her spouse identity as a wife who is involved in the relationship for emotional rather than physical reasons. At the same time, this position allows her to perceive her husband as being at the same level of sexual interest as she. The interpretation that the wife is assimilating rests on the assumption that the husband is correct and that his wife has shown no real change in her behavior. It is also possible, however, that the wife is describing accurately a transformation within herself (and possibly in the couple) but that the husband is unwilling to acknowledge this change in her. This assimilation on his part could be a consequence of his preference for seeing his wife as more sexually interested than he. Why this would be the case is not entirely clear, but it could be the outcome of a process similar to that seen in other husbands who prefer to view themselves in terms of a "negative" spouse identity. It is also possible that he simply is insensitive to the developmental shift that has taken place in his wife through her own growth in the relationship; based on a kind of "developmental envy" such as that observed in Gould's (1978) study of adult developmental phases.

These examples illustrate the tendency of spouses to transform their perceptions of the relative degree of sexual interest in the couple into a spouse identity that sees the two partners as placing equal importance on the sexual relationship. The wives in the preceding examples made this transformation even when it was obvious that the data are not consistent with their identities as spouses in relationships characterized by similarity of sexual interest.

For a number of wives, it was important to see their husbands not only as more interested than they actually were but also as the active initiators of sex, the "seducers." The assimilation involved in this process is a complicated one, involving extreme distortions and possibly deception at several levels. First, it means using assimilation to see her husband as the more active initiator of sex. In order to maintain this view of the relationship, however, the wife must eventually establish a passive role for herself in the couple's sexual relations. At the same time, though, she is still controlling the relationship indirectly by sending cues to her husband that she is in a "seducable" state. This is where the deception comes into play. By virtue of her controlling her availability to her husband, she remains in effect the one who sets the pace for the couple's sexual activities.

There is every reason to expect that, were the question to be explored, the wives who create this paradoxical situation for themselves are colluding with their husbands. Just as the wives feel it is important to their identity to be the "seductees," it is important for the husbands to maintain an image of themselves as the aggressive males in the relationship. Couples varied, of course, in the extent to which this scenario applied to them. However, the essence of this dynamic permeated the interviews of couples in both the shorter- and longer-married groups, and also those with high and low intimacy potential. Couples also varied in the extent to which they would acknowledge that the wife indirectly controlled the sexual activity of the pair. Thus, as one wife put it, the husband is the one to initiate sex "but not because I don't want to but because that's the way I enjoy it."

Another wife observed that her husband has no difficulty refusing an invitation to have sexual relations because "I think he turns over and goes to sleep. I'm not sure he realizes that I'm asking because I won't come out and say I want it." For this wife, to ask openly that the couple engage in sexual relations would violate her identity as the female being pursued by her more aggressive male partner. Redefining the meaning of "initiating," the wife in another couple observed that "I think he probably would say he does more, but I'm expecting it." In her response, this wife implies that her husband is unaware of how she indirectly controls or at least monitors the initiation of sex. The fact that she "expects" him take the initiative leaves moot the question of who is in charge in this area. The main point is that, in either event, the wife clearly does not want to take an active role in bringing about a sexual encounter.

For another couple in the longer-married group, the interactive effects of the wife's reluctance to initiate sex, in combination with a somewhat reticent husband, seem to create a no-win situation. The husband states that he has difficulty expressing himself in physical and sexual ways. The wife echoes this view about herself, but adds that she is not expressive because he is not:

So I tend to be shy about expressing some tenderness outside of what would be in bed. Even in bed I have to be the one to wait for him to start.

Her husband is aware of this, and notes that it is hard for her to initiate sex because "she tends to feel a little less like the one to start things." However, both of them seem to like it when she does take over, or at least this is his perception: "She likes it when she does it, and I like it when she does it, but it's just hard."

The husband in another couple, one of the shorter-married group, described himself as the initiator because he was following his wife's wishes:

She wants me to be assertive or aggressive and because of my shyness I look for what the reaction is going to be before acting. Sometimes I wish she would be more aggressive.

Having to take on this role bothers him, he says, because he worries about being rejected, an ever-present danger when one is made to feel solely responsible for the initiation of what is obviously a mutual process.

Along with the wife's spouse identity as being married to a partner who is sexually more interested than herself goes a tendency to assimilate the husband's behavior to the view that he is responsive to her sexual needs. In some couples, this tendency took the form of the wife's asserting that her husband was aware of her sexual preferences and insisting that he tried to accommodate them. The husbands, in these cases, said they were not aware of any preferences on the part of their wives. Another common example involved the wife insisting that the husband expressed himself in physical and sexual ways, and the husband stating that this was something he could not do. Similarly, the husband in another couple said that he holds back due to uncomfortable feelings; his wife said that he did not: "That's usually separate from the emotional." One husband who consistently stated throughout the interview that he had a great deal of trouble talking about feelings said that the same applied to the area of sexuality, that he could not talk about it easily. His wife, though, maintains that "it's probably easier for him than it is for me because he has the capacity to express himself much better than I can."

Similarly, another wife claimed that talking about sex did not bother her husband; while from his point of view it does: "I feel it must be spontaneous and I must have a mental block."

In these cases, then, wives miss seeing the difficulties their husbands face or perceive in the area of sexuality. Although it is possible that the husbands are using identity assimilation, it is more likely that the wives feel a need to present their husbands as being more sexually open and interested than they are. This allows the wives to maintain their own spouse identities as sexually desirable and attractive to their husbands.

Wives might also feel it is important to preserve a positive front for their husbands, particularly in the couples married 10 years or less, for whom the accommodation process is not as well-established. One of these wives wistfully observed that:

Sometimes I wish it would be more frequent but sometimes I get really tired and I have ambivalent feelings about it right now, so I'm not totally comfortable with it.

This discrepancy between her spouse identity and her behavior is obviously a source of concern to this wife. However, she has not yet brought this matter up with her husband. To do so, one might suspect, would be perceived by her as threatening his spouse identity as a husband who is making his wife sexually content.

Another form that this kind of assimilation takes, and this was noted in the longer-married wives exclusively, was to take on the "blame" for whatever problems the couple are experiencing. For one wife, this meant relieving her husband of any of the burden for her inability to reach orgasm during sexual intercourse. According to her, her husband "feels defensive" about this, because he feels that it is his "fault." She is unable, she maintains to "convince him otherwise." Implicit in her statement is the idea that her husband does not have or share responsibility for the dilemma the couple faces, and that she is willing to take the major share of the burden. Another couple's responses revealed a more complex version of this process. The husband stated that he has no difficulty initiating sexual relations, but the wife thinks that he does because:

I think it's easy for him to say it, but I don't think it's always easy for me to hear it...he may not express it because he thinks I'm not going to hear it.

Thus, the wife attributes greater difficulty to her husband than he expresses himself, but she then goes on to say that it is because of her unreceptiveness that he has these problems. Later, she states that she is uncomfortable talking about sex, although her husband perceives her as having no problems in this regard. The wife claims that her discomfort is not his fault; it is because "I'm uncomfortable with that." In a related vein, a wife in the longer-married group felt relieved that her husband did not place more importance on the sexual aspects of their relationship than he did. She was grateful to him because he understood her feeling that it is important but not the most important thing and because "he's always been very kind about it." What this statement implies is that her husband's ability to transcend the difference she perceives between them is deserving of her gratitude rather than being a fact of life of the relationship. The alternative, presumably, would be that she would feel blamed by him for lacking his enthusiasm toward sex, and that she would be deserving of this blame were that the case. Ironically, her husband states that he feels the emotional aspects of the relationship outweigh the physical and so he does not seem to perceive a disparity between their sexual appetites.

Other wives perceived themselves as having limitations on their part that were entirely their fault and that must perforce be a source of grave disappointment to their husbands. These reports were not verified in the statements of their husbands, who perceived no problems at all in the sexual functioning of their wives. Furthermore, no husbands attributed fully to themselves problems in the sexual relationship.

A related tendency shown by wives was to assume that their husbands were unhappier with their sexual relationship than the husband's response would indicate. Wives believed that their husbands would like their sexual activity to be more exciting than it was, that their husbands were "frustrated" that their sexual relations were not more frequent, and that, in the most extreme case, "I would say he thinks it's one of our biggest disappointments in our marital life from his point of view." The husband of this wife gave no indication of being this unhappy about the diminution of sexual activity following the birth of their second child, calling it "a very superficial sort of thing that is probably natural and expected." It is possible, of course, that the husbands in these cases give one message to their wives and another to the interviewer. Wives might then be accurately describing the situation, leaving husbands to be the ones who are using assimilation, perhaps toward deliberate ends at that. Indeed, there were a number of couples in which husbands did appear to be unjustly critical of their wives. One husband went into a long description of how unfulfilling the couple's sexual relationship is due to restrictions that his wife places upon them; he would like it to be more playful, more "filthy, dirty, playing around type stuff, to use an unclinical type thing." Furthermore, he noted, this restriction has spread to other areas of their relationship:

We don't live our lives in separate compartments, sex is not separated from the other things that go on in your life, it permeates everything else. Her feeling is definitely to get categorized or now is the time for sex, now let's forget everything that's gone on in the past, let's forget my lack of respect for your philosophy and everything and let's have a good time and have sex.

Another husband also described his wife's attitude toward sex in unflattering terms:

She has hers first and then I have mine, but she's not anxious to continue after she has her orgasm. She's ready to sanitize, get her book, and go to bed.

Thus, husbands may give their wives reasons to worry that their fulfillment of the sexual aspects of their spouse identities is less than complete. Apart from these cases involving direct blame, there were numerous instances in which husbands gave extremely negative evaluations of some aspect of their wives' attitudes toward sexuality, evaluations that did not mesh with what the wives said about themselves. In one of these couples, the wife responded to the question of who finds sex more important by responding that sex means "a little" more to her husband than to herself. Her husband's evaluation was far more harsh: "I got the feeling that she could be satisfied with never having sex again." This is a very strong statement, and so much of an exaggeration that its validity is seriously called into question. Whether it is true or not, however, it is obvious that this husband is going to be presenting a view of the relationship to his wife that is highly unflattering to her spouse identity. To the extent that she eventually accommodates to this view, she will come more and more to downgrade her degree of sexual interest.

It is always possible that the wives who present a rosier picture of their sexual interest were simply ignoring obvious facts that were apparent to their husbands and not themselves, but the nature of the comments in this category of responses suggests instead that the wives were being evaluated by harsher standards than were called for by their behavior. In one case, for example, the wife said that it was easier for her to talk about sex than her husband thought it was for her, but "I'm not sure I'm always heard." Another wife was judged by her husband to have little interest in sexual relations, but she stated that she would in fact like to have sex more often than they do. The most extreme example of a wife being unfairly evaluated was in the case of a couple in which the husband observed: "I don't know what motivates her to do or not to do." He goes on to say that he is not satisfied with the sex in their relationship and that his partner is not trying to improve the situation whatsoever: "I think if it were nonexistent she would be satisfied. I don't think she cares."

The wife, in her interview, disclosed the surprising fact that she has had five pregnancies in five years of marriage, and that therefore:

I can't exactly say we're lacking on it, although I'm sure he doesn't agree with me. When you find yourself pregnant and miscarrying, pregnant and miscarrying, and so on and so forth, enough is enough after a while.

The husband also observes that his wife does not initiate sexual relations, but as it turns out, according to her, "If I initiate it, he will negate it, although he tells me he wants me to initiate it. . . . If I initiate it, he will say no." This wife seems to be in a "damned if you do and damned if you don't" situation in which her husband judges her sexual interest as low and then actively discourages her from showing it in the form of initiating sexual activity.

The opposite sort of attribution was made by another husband, who described himself as satisfied with the type and quality of the couple's sexual relationship, but not with the quantity:

It's not often enough, but what the heck. . . . She has had menstrual troubles and in the mid-70s she went through menopause. That's one reason I haven't been pushing things.

What this husband does not realize is that his wife is very satisfied with their sexual relationship and obviously is not bothered by the "troubles" that he attributes to her. Indeed, since the interview took place over five years after the time he cited, it would appear that the husband is judging his wife's present sexual behavior on the basis of past difficulties rather than her current interest and satisfaction. Other husbands similarly did not seem to notice changes that their wives mentioned as having occurred in themselves that made them more interested and satisfied with sexual activity.

From these examples, it appears that a number of husbands were quite critical of their wives, many more than were the number of wives criticizing their husbands. Wives, in turn, made many self-derogatory comments, but no husbands did. It is plausible that there is a more pronounced tendency for wives to mold their identities in conformity with their husbands' negative evaluations of them than husbands do in response to their wives. Wives, it would appear, have far more fragile spouse identities in the area of sexuality than do husbands. A wife also can be placed in a situation in which she is made to feel defensive about her sexuality, seeing it as a reflection of her total identity as an individual. One wife stated that she did not like to turn down her husband's invitation to have sex because:

I don't like to, if I'm able to, it's not going to be a big problem. I don't ever like to give him the idea I'm just giving in to make him happy. I like to think that I can do a full-time job and a part-time job and do everything.

For this wife, being sexually active means that she is not compromising her spouse identity through her involvement in her job and "everything" else that she does. She must perceive herself as sexually active and interested in order to allow herself to continue fulfilling her identity as a worker. Were she to refuse her husband's sexual advances, this would detract not only from her spouse identity, but from her identity as a competent worker as well. The area of sexuality, then, becomes tied in with a woman's identity outside the sphere of marriage in a way not evident in the interviews of men. For a woman not to be a sexually responsive mate due to her outside commitments means that she might have to give up these involvements in order to preserve her identity within the marriage.

The only situation in which wives volunteered negative evaluations of their husbands was when the wives themselves were making critical appraisals of their own sexual interest or performance. A wife would feel free to say that her husband was less than enthusiastic about sex, found sex routine, or in some other way was not the ideal sexual partner as long as that deficiency was perceived to be identical to her own. The important point here is not whether she was accurate in her appraisal of his interest in sexuality, but the fact that negative comments were almost never volunteered outside the context of the wife's perceieved limitations.

Analysis of the assimilation processes used by husbands and wives, then, revealed that these couples held some very traditional spouse identities in the area of sexuality. Wives see themselves as having to "seduce" their men rather than being able to express their sexuality directly. The only criticisms of their husbands that they feel free to express are ones that include themselves and they freely blame themselves for difficulties in the relationship. Husbands are also likely to criticize their wives rather than themselves if there are sexual difficulties, even in extreme cases such as when there is physical illness. Given that there is so little room for a wife to maneuver in indicating her sexual interest without overstepping the prudent bounds of playing the pursued target of her man's desires, it is no surprise that wives find themselves so often to be the target of criticism. The assimilation in this process is, of course, the interpretation of these complications in terms of spouse identities based on simplistic stereotypical notions of acceptable male and female sexual behavior.

Accommodation Processes

Given the many potential areas for misperceptions that result from the traditional spouse identities held by these couples, it might seem unlikely that any accurate perceptions and agreement could exist at all. However, there was remarkably strong evidence that couples had managed to adapt to each other's identities and shared experiences in the area of sexuality. Also surprising in this regard, given the results in other areas of intimacy, was the extent to which such adaptations were made by couples regardless of the length of their marriages. In some cases, the adaptations were apparently made by wives; in other cases it was the husband whose responses expressed the result of accommodation processes. For many couples, the accommodation process was a mutual one.

For a wife to accommodate to her husband's interest in sexuality means that she must somehow overcome the tendency shown by wives in general to be unduly critical of themselves if there are difficulties in communication or disparities in their sexual appetites. For one wife, this meant perceiving accurately her husband's discomfort with variations from their standard pattern of lovemaking. Her observation agreed with her husband's admission that it is difficult for him to express himself sexually: "He thinks it's so goofy to get into all this stuff, fantasy or little things like this." This wife was not embarrassed by disclosing that her own needs for variation were stronger than those of her husband. For most wives, however, "accommodation" to the sexual experiences of the couple meant that their view of their own sexual difficulties coincided with their husbands' perceptions of them. This contrasts, in the following way, to the analogous situation in which wives use assimilation to blame themselves for sexual problems. The wife who has adopted her husband's negative evaluation of her sexual interest and behavior has adjusted her identity to take into account the feedback she gets from him. Thus, for example, a wife in the shorter-married group observed that expressing herself sexually is somewhat difficult for her, but less so for her husband because he has "less guilt feelings." Another wife commented that her husband wishes their sex life were not so routine, and this observation coincides with his response to the question. In the case of assimilation, the wife's tendency to blame herself for sexual difficulties contrasts with her husband's more neutral view of her or with his own apparent indifference to the problems she cites. Accommodation reflects, then, an incorporation into her spouse identity of the critical appraisal that her husband has made of her or of the relationship.

There are some convoluted and complicated potential relationships between assimilation and accommodation in the case of the spouse identity of wives. The accommodation process may follow a period of assimilation in which the wife alone blames herself, as she convinces the husband that it is she, not he, whose limitations are at the root of their sexual difficulties. Accommodation may also precede assimilation, in the sense that what appears to be assimilation on the part of the wife in blaming herself may represent an accommodation that had taken place in the past. The husband, having seen his wife come to adopt a negative view about her role in creating sexual difficulties, may choose not to emphasize this any longer to protect her, to keep from making her feel bad or to avoid making him appear to be a critical person. Since his identity is not scathed by his wife's appearing to be at fault, he has no particular need to point the finger at her as the cause of their problems. For her part, the wife can accept the negative evaluation of herself into her spouse identity because it still leaves intact her positive appraisal of her husband that for her forms an important part of her own spouse identity. Since her identity as a spouse rides more heavily on her positive appraisal of her husband, she has more at stake in viewing him negatively than she does in incorporating unfavorable assessments into her own identity.

For husbands, the accommodation process holds an alternate set of potential complications. Husbands feel more comfortable than do wives with adopting a critical stance toward their partners. As has just been shown, it is quite likely that wives accommodate this critical view of themselves into their own identities. When a husband perceives his wife's limitations "accurately" (i.e., in a way that agrees with what she says about herself), it could be due to either his wife having already undergone an accommodation process to his views or his wife's current assimilation of problems within the couple to her spouse identity as being the one at fault. A more "pure" form of accommodation occurs instead when a husband "accurately" perceives himself to be the one responsible for the couple's problems. This process appears to be reflected in this younger husband's correct observation about his wife that "there may be times when she wants or is more interested than I am, I'm tired and I don't respond and maybe she wants me to."

Another reasonably clear-cut case of the husband's accommodation to his wife is when he is able to predict correctly the way she would respond to a question, as in the following couple regarding the issue of who initiates sexual activity. His response was: "I think she thinks she does and I think that I think I do. In reality, the truth is somewhere in the middle." His wife does, as predicted, respond that she thinks she is the one to initiate sex more often. Her husband's analysis reflected an accommodation process, then, in that he both anticipated what she would say and was able to differentiate her position from his. His estimate of who initiates sex also has a balanced quality to it, in that he sees the "true" picture as one involving compromise.

Accommodation may also involve the correct appraisal that one's partner is unaware of one's own dissatisfaction. This was the case for a husband in the longer-married group, who stated that he did not "push things" regarding his desire to have sex more frequently. His wife was indeed unaware of his dissatisfaction with the amount of sex in the relationship. This example illustrates the point that not all husbands who are critical of their wives allow this negative evaluation to surface so that their wives must accommodate to it. On the other hand, by suffering in silence, he does not give his wife the stimulus to accommodate to his needs. However, it is also possible that this issue is not of suffcient importance to his spouse identity to lead him to make his dissatisfaction known to his wife.

The causal links in cases of one-sided accommodations obviously are difficult to interpret because, by definition, only half of the total picture can fully be examined. Mutual accommodation processes, which are defined as involving statements by spouses that are totally complementary, are less ambiguous.

In analyzing cases of mutual accommodation, the principle seems to hold that husbands who are critical of themselves can be considered "purer" cases of accommodation than husbands who accurately perceive the critical evaluations their wives make of themselves. In the case of this couple, for instance, the wife commented that her husband does not have a high sex drive: "You know, some men think about it a lot and they want it a lot; he's not that way." This observation reflected precisely the husband's self-appraisal:

I wish I was more interested in that way, and when I get the well turned in that direction I like it, it's good. Left to my own, when I don't work at it I can be pretty unromantic.

Regarding their satisfaction with the sex in their relationship, the wife sees her husband as content because: "he doesn't ask for a whole lot, he doesn't seem to yearn for too much more than we do." Again, these sentiments are mirrored precisely in the husband's own evaluation that he is satisfied because:

I haven't known to expect any more from myself than I have.... It's not quite the pie in the sky you get from thinking whatever society uses to make you think it's much better than it is, but...it's fine with me.

Although generally quite accepting of her husband's lack of enthusiasm for sex, the wife did express the regret over there not being enough "pizzazz" in the relationship. This desire is not something that she has communicated to him, because this husband gives no evidence that his wife has any complaints about his lack of interest in sexuality. Indeed, as in the previous example in which the husband had not let his dissatisfaction be made known to his wife, this husband did not seem to have accommodated negatively to his wife's perception of the relationship.

In evaluating a couple's mutual accommodation to each other, it was important to rule out cases that appeared to be accommodation (mutual agreement) because the couple had similar beliefs anyway about the importance of sexuality and their satisfaction with this aspect of their relationship. It is, of course, possible that the couple arrived at their similar views through a mutual accommodation process, but this cannot be inferred from straightforward cases of agreement. A somewhat more convincing case can be made when couples present identical perspectives on a particular issue in their sexual relationship. The partners may agree, for example, that one person initiates sex more frequently than the other, on whether they accommodate each other sexually, and on which partner finds sex more important. The responses that spouses give may complement each other, as in one couple in which the husband reported that it was not hard for him to initiate sexual activity. His wife elaborated: "We have just a little system where he would just sort of move over, touch me, we don't talk."

In other couples, there may be agreement in the way an answer is phrased, such as both partners mentioning that they switch off in accommodating to each other's preferences. Both may give a similar appraisal about whether sex is routine or exciting and cite similar reasons to account for why this varies. For example, the spouses in one couple both mentioned that this depends on how tired they are from work. Agreement may also take the form of both partners acknowledging that they feel uncomfortable talking about sex or share some other difficulty.

Even when there is agreement, the possibility remains that one partner is, in a sense, "assimilating the accommodation." That is, in order to maintain one's spouse identity, it might be necessary for that spouse to present a change imposed by the partner as one that the spouse truly desired. This is a plausible hypothesis for the case of the wife whose husband had initiated an open marriage. She described herself as satisfied with their sexual relationship, adding, "I think he's even more so now that he has the experience to have another woman as well; the comparisons." It would seem that this wife "protests too much" about how much the open-marriage arrangement, which she has complained about at length elsewhere in her interview, has added to her sexual satisfaction. Thus, as this example illustrates, it is possible that what appears to be accommodation is a spouse's way of denying that the situation is less than entirely satisfactory. It is also possible for both partners to assimilate mutually some aspect of the relationship that would threaten the spouse identities of one or both partners. In one couple, husband and wife agreed that the husband was the one to initiate sexual activity. They also agreed that this was due to the wife's having undergone what she called "drastic hormone changes as a result of surgery and ovary problems." These "changes" had occurred a number of years earlier, and although it is plausible that these changes had a temporary effect, it is doubtful that his initiating sexual activity more than she is entirely due to this physical problem. It seems reasonable to suggest that for this couple both had assimilated to the same degree, and thus their "accommodation" was one that was relative to each other's experience, not the objective "reality" of their situation.

A similar problem exists in couples in which one or both partners correctly predict what each other would say but this prediction conflicts with some other response from within the interview of that couple. One pair gave evidence of this process in their evaluations of to whom sexual activity is more important. The husband claimed that it is more important to him but predicted that his wife would say it was of equal importance to both of them. This prediction of his wife's response turned out to be correct, for she did claim that sex was equally important to both of them. The wife did acknowledge, however, that her husband initiated sex more often than she did. This pair of responses proves to be extremely complicated from the point of view of the interaction it represents of the two spouse identities within the couple. The husband would appear to be correct in the sense that his wife did say what he said she would about sexual activity being of equal importance to both of them. The wife would appear to be assimilating in that if her husband initiates sex more often, it is likely that he is indeed more interested in sexual activity. Her failure to see the discrepancy between her evaluation of an equal relationship and her husband's more frequent initiation of sex would seem to qualify as assimilation. However, it is possible that the wife's perception of equality is accurate, that she is attempting to make her husband appear to be more interested for the sake of enhancing her own identity as a desirable mate. The husband's claim that sex is more important to him could represent his assimilation of their equal interest in sex to his identity as the sexually active male in the relationship. The fact that he correctly predicts her response is, then, the only certain aspect of accommodation apparent in this series of questions. Any other inferences about who "really" is correct become extremely risky in view of what has already been found about gender differences in the assimilation of sexual experiences within the marriage.

In another couple, the issue became complicated in a different way, involving multiple twists and turns around the question of the husband's potential dissatisfaction. The wife believes that the husband would prefer to have sexual relations more frequently than they do. He indeed expresses concern that their time and energy have become limited since having children. He says that what bothers him is not so much their low frequency of sexual relations, but the fact that:

She doesn't think about it at all and I try to think about how to sandwich it in now and then. She doesn't think about it and that's the rub.

Confirming this, the wife says that sex is important, but it is "not something that's on my mind." Thus, her husband is correct in his assessment of her, and her perception of her husband's view of her represents accommodation into her own spouse identity. The husband then goes on to say that he has "become more accepting" of their infrequency of sexual relations but that he does try to "guilt-trip her" on this issue. It is these cues on which his wife bases her inference that her husband is indeed upset about the situation. She herself has responded to his cues and says that she does feel guilty about not matching his level of sexual interest. It would seem that the husband is not living up to his ideal of becoming more "accepting" and that his belief that he has changed in this regard is the result of an assimilation process. However, by acknowledging that he "guilt-trips" his wife, this husband does show some indication of a degree of self-awareness and hence accommodation to the reality of their situation.

The most straightforward and compelling evidence for the mutual accommodation process as it operates over time comes from couples in which it is obvious that the couple had to make relatively serious adjustments to each other. This kind of process is implied in the responses of one couple married over 10 years, in which the husband observed that sex used to be more important to him than to his wife, but that they are now equal. His wife responded that sex is equally important to both of them. In order for this couple to meet at this point of saying that they value sex equally, it is likely that they each made an accommodation until they reached a balance point. Mutual accommodation may also have a more negative effect, however, as in the case of this couple regarding the issue of who initiates sexual activity. The husband states that he bases his sexual initiative on reading his wife's cues so that, as he says, "Sometimes I'm a dummy, she'll be giving me signals that I don't see." This husband has incorporated into his spouse identity the perception that he is at times a "dummy" who cannot interpret his wife's wishes. His wife claims that she has to help him at times in this domain, as she says "sometimes I'll just take him by the hand." According to her, it is sometimes difficult for him to figure out what she actually does want because "he's never sure about me." This is an ambiguous statement and can be interpreted two ways. Either the wife sees herself as someone who is not good at communicating her needs, or she is faulting her husband for not being able to detect her level of arousal or interest at any given moment during their sexual interactions. The accommodation, then, is not clear-cut, but there does seem to be a shifting in both of the spouses' identities based on their sexual communication. The husband has arrived at a more negative view of himself. The wife, perhaps, has some insight into how waiting for her husband to initiate sex places a strain on him either because of his own limitations or because of the ambiguity of her signals.

A final observation on the process of mutual accommodation and its importance to marriage comes from the analysis of the factors that contributed to satisfaction with marriage. In analyzing the similarity scores of couples according to length of marriage, it was apparent that subgroups could be formed of those couples in which both partners stated that they were satisfied and accurately perceived the other partner to be satisfied, and couples in which there was not this mutual awareness of satisfaction by both partners. The results of this analysis, shown in Table 6 of Appendix D and discussed in Chapter 3, were that among the couples married longer than 10 years, the condition of mutual satisfaction and mutual awareness of satisfaction was associated with higher marital adjustment for the husbands. This concordance of views was not predictive of marital adjustment for wives, nor was it associated with higher marital adjustment in the husbands married 10 years or less. What the finding represents is that accommodation to each other's views in the sexual domain is the only feature of marriage identified in this study that predicts marital adjustment in longer-married husbands. It would appear that by being able to make the many mutual adjustments to each other sexually, and possibly by overcoming traditionally stereotyped views of husbands and wives, couples are able to foster the marital adjustment of the husband. That this interpretation is correct is reinforced by some of the observations of husbands in the group married over 10 years, who of all people in the study were most likely to mention sexuality as an important feature of a close relationship. One of these husbands described himself as "sexually in love" with his wife, and saw his relationship as close because:

I don't know if I'd define any relationship as being particularly close if it doesn't involve sex, so that means I have a close relationship with one person.

For another husband, romance and sex are part of a good relationship according to his definition, as was the case for one of the other husbands in this group:

I don't have a sex life, I have a love life; ... being in the military I see a real difference between love and sex. Love is what you have with your wife and sex is what you go and pay $20 for.

For these husbands, then, mutual accommodation in the area of sexuality may be the most central feature of their marital adjustment because it represents their success as loving husbands in fulfilling the emotional and physical needs of their wives.

Analyses of the intimacy interview questions concerning sexuality add to the observations in other areas that husbands and wives differ substantially in the content of their spouse identities. Husbands attempt to view themselves as having a high degree of sexual interest and proficiency consistent with their spouse identities as romantic males. Problems in the sexual area are attributed to lack of enthusiasm on the part of their wives. Wives, in attempting to bolster the positive spouse identities of their husbands, accommodate to this view even though it means assuming some unflattering qualities themselves. Even when couples accommodate to each other's identities in the sexual domain, it is within this context of very traditional views about what constitutes appropriate psychological qualities of husbands and wives.

7
The Role of Communication

Most academic and lay experts on marriage agree that of all the factors that contribute to a viable relationship, good communication is the most central. In the present study, there was no overall relationship between marital adjustment and the quality of communication as judged by the rating of the actual discourse between partners when asked to solve a problem jointly.

The communication data, although not predictive of marital adjustment, nevertheless provides a rich alternative source of data about the quality of these couples' marriages, and about the relationship between identity and intimacy processes. In this chapter, we will examine in depth a number of transcript excerpts from the problem-solving task. These excerpts illustrate dramatically the qualities that differentiate between couples who communicate well and couples for whom communication is an area of difficulty.

The problem-solving excerpts also provide a unique opportunity to compare what spouses say about each other in the intimacy interview with the way they present themselves in what comes closer to a real-life reflection of their interaction (albeit in the presence of a tape recorder). This sort of external, more "objective" material serves as an important source of validating inferences about the identity processes made from self-report statements alone. Such validation can be seen in the interaction of one of the couples married over 10 years, a couple in which it was evident that the husband's spouse identity was a negative one, as described in Chapter 3. This negative identity is expressed right in the opening statement that he made in the problem-solving task:

Oh boy, now what was that again? A five-minute discussion on something that has been bothering us lately? Do you want to give me that title again for a minute? (he yells to interviewer). Okay. An issue or concern that has been bothering us lately. "You," I guess, means "us," or one of us. Now it shouldn't be hard for you to think of something about me that's been bothering you lately.

Surprisingly, and especially so given that this husband was convinced in his intimacy interview that his wife had very angry feelings toward him, the wife did not respond to this invitation to criticize her husband. Instead, she pointed out that:

It's not just you and me. It's the whole thing. The whole family thing, isn't it?....
The kids, particularly M.; ...the accident; I don't know what she's doing.

The husband, however, was not so easily distracted from looking for a disagreement. He responded:

Husband: Okay. What's she doing with her life or, what do you want to
           discuss about that? I suppose we're definitely not too much in
           agreement on even what the problem is, let alone how to go
           about doing anything about it.... I think probably...my
           main worry about it is why she, is she ever going to be able to
           drive now? Is that a concern to you or what?
Wife: No, it's not. I think she can drive, but she doesn't have any
           transportation to go to work.
Husband: ...I know what you're feeling there is that she should buy a
           car.
Wife: And where is the money?

The husband assumed, first off, that the couple will not agree about what
the problem is with their daughter. He then went on to presume that his
wife was hinting that they should buy their daughter a car. They went on to
talk about money problems, and having to pay the insurance. The husband
asked: "So, you'd probably be happy if you got some more money from me,
right?" Again, this question has a ring of defensiveness about it, with the
implication that the husband expected his wife to criticize him about his
ability to earn money. In this interaction, as in her own intimacy interview,
his wife presented herself in a radically different manner than one might
expect from her husband's portrayal of her. It is possible, of course, that
the wife is putting up a false front for the purpose of impressing the interviewer.
Even if she was more negative than she appears here, though, it
still would remain the case that her husband was continually setting up the
situation so as to maximize the negative features of their interaction. His
spouse identity, then, is clearly reflected in his style of communicating with
his wife.

   This comparison of the problem-solving excerpt with the intimacy interview
provides an excellent illustration of how the spouse identity processes
influence the couple's communication style. When relevant, as in the case
of this couple, the problem-solving excerpts will be compared with what
spouses said about themselves in the intimacy interview.

   It should be noted, however, that it was only among the shorter-married
couples that a connection existed between a couple's explicitly mentioning
communication as an important feature of a good relationship (Question
39 in the intimacy interview) and the scores received by the couple on the
joint problem-solving task (see Table 8 of Appendix D). Because of this
difference, we will examine the transcripts on the basis of the years-married
grouping of couples.

Couples Married 10 Years or Less

The fact that a relationship existed among these couples between their citing of communication as an important feature of a good relationship and their actual communication scores suggests that for these couples, good communication involves a conscious and deliberate effort. Analysis of the transcript excerpts from the problem-solving task for couples differing in communication scores shows, in addition, a number of other qualities that seem related to the ability to communicate in a constructive fashion. The process of identifying these factors will begin with analyzing the transcripts of the couples with communication problems.

Couples with Low Communication Scores

The first of these couples engaged in the following dialogue concerning the problems in their relationship:

Husband: How about sex?
Wife: I'd rather discuss teeth grinding.
Husband: Okay. Teeth grinding. Would you define that as an issue above and beyond sex?
Wife: I think it's an annoying habit. From the list I think it would qualify as,
Husband: My issue is a little bit more profound.
Wife: Which is yours?
Husband: The sex thing.
Wife: That may be more profound but I think it's minor to you,
Husband: Okay, fine.
Wife: because it's not annoying to you.
Husband: Okay, sure. Let's discuss teeth grinding.
Wife: The issue is you grind your teeth and I find it annoying.
Husband: Uh huh.
Wife: And attempts to change that behavior, I don't know if you've made any attempts to change that behavior.
Husband: Uh huh.
Wife: As a matter of fact, I think it's greatly increased lately. You used to,
Husband: Have you tried negative reinforcement? No, that's not right, have you tried punishment?
Wife: Negative reinforcement?
Husband: Yeah, like electronic grids in the mattress.
Wife: I don't think you really want to change the behavior, so I'm about frustrated with my attempts to get you to change, to get you to stop doing that.
Husband: So, what's your next step?
Wife: Divorce. No, I really don't, what do you think I should do? Do

you want to change that behavior? Is it something you want to explore?

The couple then goes on to discuss ways that the husband could change his behavior, and in the process he suggests that he looks at the "environment" for a reason. He points out that he used to bite his nails:

Husband: Remember when I bit my nails the most?
Wife: No.
Husband: When I read books. When I was studying, I was reading.
Wife: Now that you're totally illiterate.
Husband: Well now, it's not a, well, not just reading....

The reasons for this excerpt being rated as low in communication should be quite obvious. Furthermore, it is clear that it is mainly due to a combination of the wife's nonconstructive problem-solving methods combined with the husband's mildly mocking manner that the couple's communication was rated as low. The wife's nonconstructive style is illustrated first by her managing to steer the conversation to a problem that her husband must change rather than the sexual problem, one that would involve both members of the couple. She escalated the conflict when she introduced the idea (albeit in what is probably meant to be a humorous vein) of divorce as a solution. Almost immediately, she attempted to make up for this by retreating to an exploratory mode, perhaps for the benefit of the tape recorder, and this almost succeeded. However, she soon returned to her earlier critical style, even throwing in a gratuitous insult about her husband's leisure habits. The husband's flippancy, in view of all these onslaughts by his wife, is probably more of a defensive reaction than callousness. No doubt, though, his attitude further infuriated his wife who then became more extreme in her remarks.

This excerpt also illustrates one of the ways that identity assimilation operates in marital interactions. In the opening lines of this excerpt, the wife chose not to talk about sexual difficulties, and then quickly forgot that her husband even raised the problem as one worthy of discussion. This would seem to qualify as an example of denial, a form of identity assimilation. Furthermore, it is apparent that the husband quite readily conceded to his wife's desire to talk about his teeth grinding instead of the original problem he raised. In the intimacy interview, the husband had accurately described himself, at least in terms of this excerpt, as being the one to "retreat" during an argument. He described his wife as the one who "tries to confront and talk about it." She clearly is confronting the problem (his problem) in this excerpt. However, the wife's identity, as expressed in the intimacy interview, is of herself as the retreating spouse. Her spouse identity, in view of the communication excerpt, would seem to represent her effort to assimilate her more confrontive behavior to her identity as the spouse who concedes to her husband.

For another couple, the complaints that each makes about the other were tinged with far more overt hostility:

Wife:	What's bothering me?
Husband:	Okay, yeah, what's bothering you.
Wife:	The TV set. This thing. I think you watch that too much.
Husband:	I do?
Wife:	Yeah. Like I never mentioned it to you.
Husband:	(laughs).
Wife:	That thing.
Husband:	I think the same about you and your books.
Wife:	Yeah, but my books aren't distracting you.
Husband:	Yeah, they are.
Wife:	How?
Husband:	It distracts me that you can be so tied up into the book.
Wife:	So, what's wrong with that? When you can watch a mindless, idiotic program. At least I pick up a book by choice. I don't have what's thrown at me on the stupid TV set which usually is a bunch of crap. So there's one. We didn't resolve it, but,
Husband:	We'll never resolve it until Barbara (his wife's name) gets so pissed one day that she throws something through the television set.
Wife:	No. When it breaks again, 'cause once that one breaks, it's caputs and I'm not going to buy a new one.
Husband:	I am.
Wife:	Then you're going to watch one of the two black and whites.
Husband:	No. I'll buy a new one. Hands down.
Wife:	I'm going to close the charge account. I'd like to see you do it. How are you going to do it without a charge card?
Husband:	I've got a charge card. I've got one worth five thousand dollars in my pocket.
Wife:	When the TV breaks so does the charge card.
Husband:	(laughs). You've gotta get it out of my wallet, baby.
Wife:	No I don't. I just have to call it in stolen and when you go and try to charge,
Husband:	(laughs). I can see, I can call you from jail, Barb, you told them my charge card's stolen.
Wife:	Hey, I told you not to charge,
Husband:	(laughs).
Wife:	Oh well, next, ...what do we talk about? What's the third thing? Moving?
Husband:	Money (laughs).
Wife:	Money.
Husband:	Money's tight. It won't move.
Wife:	I know. We need more to buy a house, that's all.

Husband: Yeah.
Wife: No, the only thing is we have to try and budget like everyone else does when we pick up a mortgage.
Husband: That scares me.
Wife: You're weird.
Husband: Why am I weird? It scares me, the idea of a mortgage.
Wife: Well, everybody else has them.

Throughout this excerpt, the couple's angry statements and criticisms are muted by laughter, at least on the part of the husband. It appears that this couple, though they have a low communication score, probably get along better than their score indicates because of the overt as well as implied humor evident at least in this taped exchange. However, this seems to be true more for the wife than the husband. It is the husband's marital adjustment score that is relatively low, not the wife's. Looking at this transcript with that information in mind, and assuming this is representative of the couple's typical dialogues, it is possible to see the source of his low adjustment. The wife begins the exchange by directly attacking the husband's habits, and adds to this a sarcastic observation ("Like I never mentioned it to you.") Although he laughs as he creates the ridiculous scenario of his being thrown in jail for using a stolen charge card, this laughter might be seen as nervous and defensive. At the end of the exchange, his wife calls him "weird" when he exposes his fear about incurring a large debt. His scores on the intimacy interview revealed that he had a higher intimacy potential than his wife. For her part, the wife regarded herself as "spoiled," as having the ability within the marriage to "get my way a little bit more often." Although the husband stated that "sometimes you want to strangle her," the wife regarded him as "a nice guy" who will "put up with me when I'm in these moods." In the transcript excerpt, it was possible to see how he indeed "put up with" her through humor, but that there was also a considerable degree of resentment ("you gotta get it out of my wallet, baby"). It was in the sexual area of the intimacy interview, however, that this couple's largest differences emerged. The wife made numerous references to the "animal"-like sexual drives of men, and the martyr-like existence of women who must suffer in silence. The husband referred in passing, in another part of the interview, to the sex-role stereotype that he does not like to go shopping with his wife because "that's what women like to do." It is possible to speculate that to the extent that this wife's spouse identity is premised on these views of men and women, it creates a major source of interference for communication to be established between the partners. The husband, to the extent that his spouse identity is premised on similar ideas, contributes to this blocking of the open and honest exchange of feelings.

    For another couple in this group, the wife's complaint about her husband's pipe smoking stimulated an almost equally unprofitable exchange:

Husband: Ah, go ahead. Irritating habits.

Wife: Yeah, that really, your pipe smoking really bothers me. I think when it comes to other things, you're pretty good. It's just that irritating habit.

Husband: Just smoking.

Wife: Your smoking. Sometimes you sit in front of the television with your back to me, like you're closing out the whole world.

Husband: Not the whole world. You in particular. That's not the whole world. The whole world's watching TV with me.

Wife: Would you be willing to stop your smoking?

Husband: No, Yeah, maybe, sure, someday. Well, you know, I have to do it when I'm ready, and I'm just not ready. Things aren't settled down yet. . . . Too much pressure. I'm trying to do all these things and I'm not really happy yet because we're spinning wheels here.

Wife: Well, that will straighten out.

Husband: . . . The only thing that ever bothered me is you went to sleep on the couch all the time. You don't do that much anymore.

Wife: I don't do that anymore.

Husband: Really, sometimes you get on Jimmy a little too stiff. That's just because, I don't know, maybe I'm just a little too lax. We have a different relationship. Both of us are different.

Wife: A different type. I think (also) that communication still is between you and I,

Husband: That's probably our worst thing, you're right.

Wife: I think some of it's not, but we just know each other's thinking so much.

Husband: I said that earlier. That's what I thought.

Wife: That we tend not to talk, but we do need to.

Husband: The answer is communication skills. Okay, we're done (calling to interviewer in next room), we're not unhappy now!

As in the excerpts of the previous couples, this couple have committed a number of the classic "dont's" of marital communication. Rather than defining a problem that they both face as a couple, each attempts to think of ways that they irritate each other. The wife begins the discussion by stating that her husband "is pretty good," thereby transforming the problem-solving task into a more or less global evaluation of him as a spouse. Another point evident from this excerpt is that the husband has no real serious intention of complying with his wife's request. His evasive "No, yeah, maybe, sure, someday" would give only the most incurable optimist reassurance that he is about to make an effort to change his habit. The wife, for her part, then disregards her husband's expression of dissatisfaction ("we're all spinning wheels here") without taking his concerns seriously. Finally, when they agree that their communication is not all that it could be, the husband abruptly ends the dialogue with an ostensibly false and therefore unhelpful resolution.

There were other comments made by the partners together in this joint situation that corroborate statements they each made individually in the intimacy interviews. Both husband and wife agreed in this excerpt that they know what the other one is thinking without having to communicate. Each partner had made this same observation in their separate interviews. The wife had said that her husband could "pick up on" her moods, and he had said that she knows what is bothering him "and how to correct it before I even say anything." Furthermore, the wife had lamented that her husband closes her out during an argument by turning his back to her and watching television. This observation is not challenged by him but is transformed through a rough sort of humor into a criticism of her. It is clear from this excerpt that the wife was perfectly accurate in her answers given during the intimacy interview. This concordance between the individual interview and joint discussion further reinforces the inference that the wife has begun to accommodate to the reality of having a husband who shuts her out of his problems. The communication excerpt also shows, however, that the husband's movement away from his wife may be a predictable response to the wife's disregard of her husband's expression of feelings.

The wife's movement away from her husband due to his reluctance to share problems was observed in another couple with poor communication. This couple had one of the lowest sets of marital adjustment scores. The husband had said in his interview that a good relationship consists of "unsaid commonality," like the way he felt when looking at girls in seventh grade. This unsaid commonality makes speech unnecessary. In the excerpt from their problem-solving task, it is clear that the couple has translated this reluctance to communicate into an avoidant style of conflict resolution. This can be seen even at the beginning of their discussion, which opened with a vague and abstract reference to visits to elementary school with their daughter, Abby. This preliminary discussion, introduced by the husband, had almost nothing to do with the couples' assigned task of finding a problem to discuss and attempt to resolve.

Husband: What did you think about the schools that you visited recently?
Wife: The schools, the elementary schools Abby and I went to?
Husband: Yeah.
Wife: We didn't see anything but the hall and the office. So I,
Husband: You didn't meet any of the children?
Wife: No, we didn't, we were only, in the one school we went to the superintendent's office and the other school we just went to the office, so we didn't see any. We didn't go there. You have any problems?
Husband: Oh, at least five dozen I can name, but besides that (laughs).
Wife: Gosh, I can't believe after, I mean after all, I mean, you know,

for four, I usually come up with five topics, with five things I'm mad at you about but in the last couple of months it's been really nice. The only thing that's bothering me is I get scared sometimes about what's going on at work.

Husband: Oh yeah. That business has always been crazy. Probably always will be crazy, for about another 10 years it will be crazy and about that time it's time to get, another 10 years is all it's good for. 'Cause in another 10 years it will all be done.

Wife: What, work?

Husband: Yeah, that sort of work is good for about another 10 years, before it becomes mundane work, routine work.

Wife: I just get concerned because sometimes you come home at night and you're so frustrated and I can't seem to, the best I've learned, you've never come right out and said this, but I think I've learned the best thing to do is just leave you alone. Yes.

Husband: There you go.

At this point, the wife switched from indirect statements about how she worries about her husband's work to a direct attack of his avoidant communication style. The husband's response "There you go," is equally critical, implying that she is about to launch a familiar and unnecessary discussion in which he would prefer not to participate. She replies:

I'm working hard on it, but I guess I still get real, I get real concerned about it, especially now 'cause I like what I'm doing right now and if anything happens to what you're doing right now I might not be able to keep doing what I'm doing right now.

This response indicates her identity as a spouse in a parallel relationship, in that her main worry about his becoming bored with work is what would happen to her, not that he would be unhappy. The husband, feels, though that her reaction is "fair enough," and as he goes on to explain:

I keep telling you why I don't like to discuss it [his job] a lot is that half of what I do is sit in boring meetings listening to people's complaints. It's that and the next thing, what they want: I want this, I want that, why isn't this this way, why isn't that that way? I don't know, it's nice to have a little peace.

The husband seeks "peace," then, in his relationship rather than a chance to talk to his wife about how boring he finds his job. His wife finds this to be a satisfactory arrangement:

I guess I would learn to quit worrying because if you really weren't happy and something was really gonna happen then you should just quit worrying about it until you decide to drop the bomb. But, I guess, what concerns me is a couple of times the bomb did drop, like last November, October, when you said "Hey, you've got to do something, you've got to get a job," and I really didn't have enough lead time into that to know. Do you understand? Am I making any sense? I don't know, I just get concerned about that.

Throughout this interaction, the supposed intent of which was to discuss a "problem," the couple has actually been talking themselves out of an immediate problem. The wife says she "should learn to quit worrying." Although she still apparently feels resentful about her husband's possible intrusion into her own job situation (referring to his behavior as "dropping the bomb"), she attempts to neutralize this into a "concern" rather than something that upsets her. Furthermore, the fact that she defined her husband's announcement of his wish to change jobs as a "bomb" indicates her (and probably his) general aversion to bringing up negative topics. On the other hand, it is possible that since her husband does avoid telling her about minor difficulties, he leaves things unsaid until they truly are inescapable. At that point, the problem really does, from his wife's point of view, come from nowhere to explode into what had appeared to be a calm horizon. This interpretation of the sequence of events is bolstered by the wife's responses to questions in the intimacy interview about problems in the relationship. This was the wife who, as reported in Chapter 2, described her husband's preference to keep problems to herself and her reaction to this as follows:

Left alone when he's having a hard time, and after six years I'm finally learning ways to leave him alone without feeling hurt and going crying in a corner.... I try to get him to talk about it but I'm not sure if he likes that.

The husband, it was noted, had low intimacy potential, and it appeared that his wife had begun to accommodate her spouse identity in response to this. The communication excerpt reinforces this observation and illustrates exactly how the behaviors described by the couple in their interview translate into their actual interactions with each other. Furthermore, the wife's plaintive questioning of her husband at the end of this excerpt ("Do you understand?") suggests the degree to which she must struggle to get through to her husband's seemingly impenetrable shell.

Another of the couples married 10 years or less with low scores on the communication index had given many hints in their intimacy interviews of difficulties in this area. Regarding practical tasks, the husband noted that:

You communicate to one another without communicating and if something needs to be done, it gets done. We both cut the grass. We don't discuss who is going to do it, we just do it.

This bleak observation corresponds precisely to that of his wife, who implied that the problem is a chronic one:

Previously he was home during the day with the children and I was at work and he would go to work in the evenings and I would be home, so we spent most of our time doing the child-care routine and not so much in terms of our interaction with each other.

At the end of his interview, the husband lamented the lack of communication that the couple currently faces:

Communication is the most important thing in marriage. . . . If you stop communicating, then there's nothing to be close about at all. How can you be close?

Clearly, the husband acknowledges the existence of a serious problem. What he does not realize is the way the couple's communication problems translate into their interactions with each other. The excerpt from the problem-solving task revealed that both he and his wife have major gripes about how their partners relate to the children in the family. These gripes reflect a deep division within the family that shatters the core of the marital relationship. Billy (the youngest) is closer to the wife, and this is a source of consternation to the husband who in turn is allied with daughter Jessica on this issue. The wife, for her part, complained bitterly about the father's close relationship with a third child, Kim. The husband began the excerpt as follows:

There's a big issue that came up with my discussing Billy with Jessica in regard to the raising of Billy. Jessica feels that you are very tolerant as far as Billy is concerned. That's putting it mildly. You cannot imagine how Billy's actions when you are around annoy other people as much as other people feel they should annoy you. And that in everything you do you literally live for Billy. When Billy's around nobody else is to you and it's so apparent to everybody else, to everyone, that it's ridiculous. I mean, Jessica agreed and I agree. You know, Jessica doesn't agree with me about anybody. I'll say black and she'll say white, but I was amazed at that conversation. That when Billy and you are together there is no room for anybody else. That your entire being is devoted to him, and that no matter what he does it doesn't matter. And she sees what is happening and she wants to do something about it but can't. So do I, but I don't. I threaten all the time but I never do anything.

The wife, in turn, complained about him: "But you don't see that you do some of the same things with Kim." Defending himself, the husband went on:

No, no, you keep saying that and even Jessica does not feel that that's the case. When Kim asks me for something I tell her to go pick it up herself, and she does. I mean, if she bothers me I'll tell her to go away. I've told her that a million times. You don't see her climbing over me, hanging all over me. . . .

Then the wife counterattacked by pointing out how the husband ignores her supposed favorite, Billy. The conversation then proceeded as follows:

Wife: Do you see what you do to Billy?
Husband: No. I see that what Billy does is so upsetting to me that it's alienating me from him.
Wife: The other night you said to Kim, who was lying on the floor, "Kim, do you want to come sit on my lap?" She said,
Husband: Well?
Wife: She said, "I'm fine right here." Billy said, "Daddy, can I sit on your lap?" You said "No."

Husband: Billy sits and hangs all over you all night.
Wife: But he wanted to sit with you and you said "No."
Husband: Okay, now that you bring it up,
Wife: And that's not the first time.
Husband: Now that you bring it up, I see that. Okay. But I am so angry
           with Billy, and Jessica, I keep bringing up Jessica because I'm
           amazed that she agreed. I mean, I was shocked that she felt
           this way. She never agrees with me. I mean, never. No matter
           what. I think she's devoted her life to disagreeing with me. But
           when it comes to Billy and you, she's 100% in accord with me.
           She's amazed.

From this excerpt, it is possible to spot a number of serious communication
difficulties that characterize this couple. In the first place, the husband uses
Jessica to ally himself against the coalition of the wife and Billy. His criticism
of his wife comes out in the words of Jessica, and indeed he seems to be
hiding behind his daughter in this process. The wife then counterattacks by
bringing up Kim's relationship to her father. This proves to be just as
nonproductive a route to pursue, and the husband retaliates with his claim
that Billy "hangs all over you all night." The wife, continuing her attack,
notices a bit late that her husband is beginning to concede. However, before
he completes his concession (and perhaps because he was interrupted in
this process), he then goes on to defend himself once again by using his
daughter to bolster his criticism of his wife. Throughout the excerpt, in
addition to these problems, there is the highly accusatory tone taken by
both spouses, who frame their comments in terms of what "you" are doing
wrong in the family.

Having seen how the communication difficulties faced by these couples
make themselves manifest in the problem-solving exchanges, we shall turn
now to couples in the shorter-married group whose communication scores
were at the high end of the spectrum.

Couples with High Communication Scores

The first of these couples frequently asserted during the course of the
intimacy interview that communication is an essential feature of their relationship. In the area of sexuality, for example, the husband responded to
the question of how satisfied he is as follows:

We've periodically discussed, is this getting too routine? Is this the best time? Do
you want to try anything new?.... We've put a little effort into it and haven't just
given up if things weren't right.

As far as initiating sex, they have had to work out their own style:

You waste a lot of time waiting for all that nonverbal communication kind of stuff.
You can develop your own language or your own cues that are, that will work and
communicate what you want to communicate without being crude.

This couple has managed to translate their belief in the importance of communication into practice, as is evident in the problem-solving task, when they describe the problems in their relationship since having their child, Max:

Husband: Well, I don't know. I think that the only problem I can think of right now that's still being worked on is, uh, our time together and doing things other than taking care of Max.
Wife: Uh huh.
Husband: That we're working on it is good, but I don't think we're completely there yet.
Wife: Yeah, I think,
Husband: It's not quite just taking care of him, it's carving out a group image as opposed to a duo.
Wife: Uh huh. I think it's not as acute a problem as it was a couple of weeks ago.
Husband: Because we understand him better.
Wife: Yeah. And we have started to be more conscious about getting time for ourselves, but I agree that if we're not careful it can be, it can turn into the three of us all the time and not just, and not having any time for you and me.
Husband: Well, and the other thing that could also be a problem would be if it's the two of us but when it's the two of us that we're always going out to dinner or that kind of thing as opposed to just doing some,
Wife: Being,
Husband: Just sort of just being kind of just doing something easy and simple. You know, we have, it has to be an occasion.
Wife: Uh huh.
Husband: Which would be expensive and also, I mean, that just makes it harder to do it, if it's got to be a big deal.
Wife: Well, and then it's artificial.

This excerpt illustrates precisely the opposite kind of communication style as shown by the previous couples in that this husband and wife are resonating the same ideas in almost a unified voice. When the wife interrupts the husband or vice versa, it is to add the continuation of the other's thought. Moreover, the problem they have identified is one that is shared, not one that applies to one partner but not the other.

Other couples with high communication scores show a similar tendency to identify as their problem one that both partners face equally. They define the task on a different premise, and therefore set about to discuss it with a less critical attitude toward each other, united against a common concern. Even when the problems they identify do become more personal and potentially critical, these couples word their concerns in an entirely less accusatory manner, as in the following excerpt:

Husband: The first thing that comes to my mind is your folks.
Wife: Yeah. Maybe we should give some background information.
Husband: I mentioned it a little bit when she was interviewing me.
Wife: Did you? Oh, I didn't.
Husband: That your dad has arthritis severely, and their needing to make some decisions soon about what to do.
Wife: Yeah. Okay.
Husband: I guess I was concerned in the last phone conversation when your dad said it was difficult for him to talk on the phone and you didn't react much to that, so I wondered if you felt you were going to be further isolated from them as a consequence. Where that left things.
Wife: I was, when he said that, I think I was glad that he was able to be honest about that, and that he did, and he didn't just subordinate his feelings of hurting because he wanted to talk to us or he didn't want us to worry about him.
Husband: Or didn't want us to be disappointed in him.
Wife: Yeah, so I guess I was just really,
Husband: Relieved at his candor.
Wife: Glad that he could say that. I was disturbed because of the further deterioration of his condition. But I guess I didn't think of it in terms of "Oh, we're not going to be able to keep in contact with him." I did think of it in terms of, you know, they have those little things you can put on your shoulder to make it easier to talk on the phone.
Husband: That's what I thought of too. So he wouldn't have to hold the phone while he talks.
Wife: Just prop the phone up to his face. I thought maybe it would be nice to look for one of those for him, not just for talking to us but for talking with anybody.
Husband: In general. That was one thing that occurred to me.
Wife: I'd like to look and see if we could find one of those....
Husband: Yeah.
Wife: But, so, I don't think that issue disturbed me as much as his deterioration.

The couple then continued the conversation, discussing various options that they might have to pursue if the wife's father becomes more debilitated and in need of nursing care. They also discussed communication problems among the wife's parents and the difficulties this creates as they look for a new home. By the end of the dialogue, the wife made a humorous observation about her parents and laughs. It is clear that her husband's support of her concern had consoled and reassured her. It is also apparent from the outset of the exchange that the husband, though in a sense criticizing his wife, uses an "I" message to convey this idea. This is the type of communication method advocated by many popular and professional approaches to improving marital interactions. By framing the problem as one that comes to "my" mind, in this case, it presents the problem as one that might not be real in some absolute sense, and in that regard a criticism of her, but as a concern that "I" perceive. The husband also phrases his opening statement as "I guess I was concerned," not "You were distant on the phone with your father," which would be a more critical way to put the issue to her. The whole point of his introducing the topic, though, is to help his wife with a problem, not to point out a flaw in her behavior.

For another couple whose communication was generally constructive, the discussion does focus on what could be seen as a more negative attribute of one of the spouses. Here again, however, the discussion is framed in such a way that the spouse being criticized does not feel attacked:

Husband: Well, what's on your mind that's bothering you?
Wife: Very little's been bothering me. I get concerned, and I was expressing this to you the other night that with your new job, I guess I get concerned that you'll push yourself. You'll push yourself too hard. I mean that I understand that that's a needful push at the moment because,
Husband: Yeah,
Wife: Because of the demands of the job.
Husband: Yeah, that's right.
Wife: But I said the other night, I'm concerned.
Husband: I want to do well at this.
Wife: Oh, I know. I think you will. I guess my concern is that you're able to divorce your brain enough when you're not working that you're going to wake up in the middle of the night.
Husband: Yeah, I'm concerned about that too.
Wife: And be concerned about the nit-picking details of the job. I did, I must confess, the other night I did dream about a project I'm working on.
Husband: Well,
Wife: How's that for commitment?
Husband: Well, you've been at it longer, though, is the thing. I mean, but you're a less obsessive person though.
Wife: I know, but you're, that's why.
Husband: I was going to say, if you got the manager's job you would probably become,
Wife: I would be reasonably hysterical about that, though, initially, because it's such a big thing.
Husband: Well, I would hope so, but I don't think by our different natures that you'd be as obsessive as I
Wife: Whatever in my,
Husband: would be.
Wife: Yeah. Whatever in my head that says, that clicks things on and

off to protect me does not function as much for you, and I guess I worry when

Husband: No, it doesn't.

Wife: I look at you that you're,

Husband: But part of it, it's not so much the worry, it's the nature of having a new job. If I'm still doing this a year from now, I'd say that was a legitimate cause for concern.

What is evident in the excerpt so far is again the way a potential criticism is expressed as an "I" statement, and furthermore, how the couple both attempt to sort out the contributions of the husband's personality traits (being more of a worrier) from the situation (a new job) as contributors to his current "obsessive" attitude toward work. Furthermore, both husband and wife show a nondefensive and open attitude toward admitting that they each might have some weaknesses or problems. As the discussion continues, another major contrast becomes evident in the way that well-communicating couples resolve problems:

Wife: Well, I guess when I worry, it's the thing I was mentioning tonight that having a little more to drink than is good for you.

Husband: Well, I've been doing that for a while now.

Wife: I know, but that worries me because I don't want to see you get out of balance in a way that you have been.

Husband: Yeah.

Wife: On the other hand, the fact that you're doing something that you want to be working hard at is such a pleasant change because, I mean, you don't know how pleased I am, I guess we're not supposed to be talking about this in this part of the interview, when you come home and you tell me all about your job. I mean, how long has it been since you've done that?

The wife introduces a complaint, similar in content to that made by the other wives about teeth grinding, smoking, and watching too much television. However, this wife frames this complaint as an "I statement ("I worry") and also in a way that emphasizes that she is worried because the habit is bad for her husband's health. She then quickly moved off the topic, having stated her concern, onto a positive feature of the previous discussion, thus reframing that worry into a source of happiness.

Several of the features contributing to the high communication scores of these couples should by now be very clearly apparent. They avoid attacking each other, focus on constructive ways of solving problems, are nondefensive about their own weaknesses, and, perhaps most importantly, define problems as one that face both members of the couple. Furthermore, based on the intimacy interviews, it is also apparent that these couples regard it as important to work on and develop their ability to communicate with each other.

Couples Married Longer Than 10 Years

For these couples, the explicit recognition of the value of communication was not directly related to the couple's actual scores on the problem-solving task. The couples who communicate well with each other seem to take it as a given that this is an important feature of a good relationship. Those with poor communication scores may see the value of good communication but are unable to translate this into practice when confronted with a problem-solving situation. Another complicating factor is the emphasis given by these couples on mutual accommodation. As we shall see in the transcript excerpts of these couples, some of the least functional couples in terms of communication believed that they had accommodated so well to each other that there was no need for them to speak.

The data from the two sets of couples are cross-sectional, and so any discussion of "changes" over time in high- and low-communicating marriages becomes tenuous. However, there are some continuations of themes seen in the couples married 10 years or less than can be followed in the transcritps of the longer-married couples.

Couples with Low Communication Scores

The first couple was one of those for whom, based on the intimacy interviews, there was evidence of a considerable degree of mutual accommodation over the course of the marriage. The husband claimed that "compromise" was an important feature of a good relationship, and the wife observed that "you have to learn to put up with someone." In this dialogue between them, however, a number of problematic areas appear.

Wife: Well, Steve, we've arranged for the child-care issues, sexual issues are all taken care of, even to do more housework, more house fixing up. I hate to be leader (laughs). All right, what else? In-laws are basically no problem, moving is not a problem, vacation plans are not a problem. We need to make more. You agree with all that. Who needs to argue?

Husband: It certainly showed you talk a lot (they both laugh).

Wife: Oh, Steve, it's such a bad habit. You're too flip.

Husband: I'm too flip?

Wife: Flip, flip. It's very serious, isn't it? (laughs) I told her we didn't have any problems.

Husband: You should hear what I told her.

Wife: Did you tell her, did you tell her problems? In-law? Child rearing? Such? Your sister, we could rehash that. That warranted a good fight. I told her we never fight. All right, you just walk away for a few minutes, if anything (both laugh). What else is problems? You're not saying much.

Husband: What's the problem? There's no, we can always use more money, we can always use time with each other.

Wife:	We'll have that when the children are gone.
Husband:	Right. We'll really find out if we like each other.
Wife:	That's all we have to say. We've enjoyed the same friends mostly. Crazy kids, that's all. You call her this time (referring to interviewer).
Husband:	No, you call her.
Wife:	I called her the last time. Call her this time, Steve.
Husband:	(silence).
Wife:	Very interesting.
Husband:	We're pretty dull. We're finished.
Wife:	We're done, Joyce.

In this interchange, the husband begins by criticizing the wife for talking too much, a charge which she counters with a criticism of him for being too "flip." They laugh off this dispute. The husband then teases his wife about all the problems he told the interviewer. In fact, he had told her that they do not really fight: "we've matured to the point that we think it's [fighting] not worth it." However, in this problem-solving task, he pretends to have made their situation sound far more serious. This makes his wife nervous but the husband does nothing to reassure her. Finally, at the end of the excerpt, there is a power struggle over who will call the interviewer back into the room. Indeed, throughout this exchange, the husband has virtually signed off from talking about difficulties at all. Despite the couple's assurances that they had in fact accommodated to each other, then, this excerpt reveals that their situation is not an ideal one in terms of the way they actually do relate to each other.

For another couple, whose marital adjustment was also relatively high, a major disagreement transpired in the course of their problem-solving task over the cleaning of the house. The wife had, in her intimacy interview, alluded to her husband's being more concerned than she with the upkeep of the house: "If it isn't cleaned enough to his satisfaction, he would certainly point it out." She also felt that she had accommodated to her husband's personal qualities:

After 11 years, I'm still in love with him, which is nice. I don't always agree with him, I probably see more of his faults than I ever saw 2 years ago, not 2, let's say 10 years, even 2, yeah, and I really care about him, where he's going and I'm committed to have him find what he wants in life.

She thinks about the relationship, she says, with "some awareness," at least what he probably would like "whether he's getting it or not...that he likes things dusted." Obviously, this wife is very concerned about the quality of her housekeeping. Indeed, in their problem-solving discussion, this is exactly the issue that her husband brings up:

Husband:	What burning issue has come up for you that you would want to discuss at this point? That you aren't happy with?

Wife: I can't think of any right off, can you?
Husband: Hum. The condition of the house.
Wife: You mean housekeeping?
Husband: Housekeeping. Yes.
Wife: Oddly enough, that doesn't bother me. What more do you want me to do? Do you want to do some other things?
Husband: Yeah. I'd like to see if we could resolve that issue with you pretty much picking up after yourself.

They then engaged in a dispute about whether or not she picks up after making lunches for the children:

Husband: In the morning, when you leave, the kitchen's a mess. I usually clean it up.
Wife: The only reason the kitchen is a mess, I don't eat in the morning, all I do is make your lunches. Would you rather not have me make your lunch? Or the children's?
Husband: Okay, we know what the problem is, what can we do to clear it up?
Wife: I could not make lunches and you could make the lunches and clean up afterwards and then you're not faced with a mess afterwards.

The husband then tentatively suggested that the wife simply "wipe things," which initiated the following exchange:

Wife: I usually do.
Husband: No you don't.
Wife: What don't I wipe down? I use one counter and I wipe it down afterwards. . . . I do wipe it down. I can't do anymore than I've been doing. I've been consistently making sure I do one swipe over it, because I know it's one thing that you'll be unhappy with.
Husband: I don't think it does any good to talk about all the little items because you could sit here forever and name them all.

Rather than drop the issue, though, the wife interrupted with "And it's the kitchen in the morning." This stimulated the husband to suggest, again, that "there's little things you can do to clean up most of the things." When he asserted again that he is the one to clean it up, the wife retorted with a criticism of the quality of his work:

Wife: What do you do? You don't put the bread away, because I do. You don't put the cookies away, because I do. You haven't been putting the plastic bags away because I've done that and I know I have. You can't tell me I didn't do it this morning.
Husband: That's right. You did. Yeah, you did.
Wife: So, did you have anything to clean up this morning? From me?

This rhetorical question then stimulates her husband to maneuver around his previous admission.

Husband: The table.
Wife: I didn't do anything on the table.

This failing, he then switches again: "I swept the floor." The wife was not put off by this change of topics, and she restated her position:

No, we're talking about lunches and what you clean up after me. You didn't clean up the table for me. I don't use it in the morning. What I'm saying is, are you being realistic in your asking me to do this when I'm not doing it anyway? The kids come down and eat breakfast.

The husband then admitted his wife is correct, but added to this a renewed criticism:

Husband: I'm probably not being realistic in asking you because I know
             that's not going to solve it.
Wife: What's going to solve it is you saying,
Husband: Me doing it.
Wife: Is your doing it, but what did you have to do this morning
             from me making lunches? You did not have to clean up that
             counter.

The wife, restating her victory, was probably not prepared for her husband's next comment, which once again shifted the ground they were covering to one that might reflect on him more favorably.

Husband: You qualified this. You narrowed it down to one little aspect.
             I'm talking about everything in general.
Wife: Okay, what's everything in general?
Husband: The dishes in the sink, the stuff on the floor.
Wife: Okay, since when does everybody else have broken arms in
             this house?
Husband: Well, obviously, my arms haven't been broken for days. I've
             been cleaning up.

Now it was the wife's turn to shift the territory.

Wife: Have you ever cleaned a toilet?
Husband: Not recently.
Wife: Not in this house you haven't.
Husband: Yes I have.
Wife: In this house?

Particularly intriguing about this dialogue is the way in which the partners parry their comments, shifting and reshifting the topic of concern so as to gain the most advantage over each other. They seem to have honed their destructive problem-solving methods to a fine degree. Both partners appear to be aware of the rules and to use them to their maximum advantage in order to score as many points as possible.

The general tenor of the conversation contrasts sharply with the identities of both spouses in this marriage as people who are "resolving" their problems. Furthermore, the wife's neutral observation that if her husband noticed something wrong he would "point it out" conflicts sharply with the critical manner in which he actually directs his comments. This couple, then, have identities as partners in a smoothly functioning relationship, but their method of resolving a problem calls the reality of this belief sharply into question.

Among the longer-married couples with low communication scores were several who simply could not fill up the five minutes alotted to them for the problem-solving task. This situation may have developed as the result of years of avoidance of painful issues or due to lack of practice. Both of these possibilities seem likely on the basis of the following excerpt.

Husband: Go ahead, discuss dear.
Wife: I don't want to talk about the living room sofa.
Husband: So don't talk about the living room sofa.
Wife: I know that's been bothering us.
Husband: Fine.
Wife: We had the car.
Husband: Why is that between the two of us? That's between me and my car.
Wife: No. Should we buy a new car when I have to drive it?
Husband: You don't have to drive it.
Wife: I drove it all last week.
Husband: That was unusual. Besides, I'm going to get it fixed.
Wife: Okay. That boring anyway (laughs).
Husband: (laughs). I can't think of anything that's been bothering us, between the two of us.
Wife: Well, just time.
Husband: Well, but that's not recent. That's always. . . . There isn't anything that's not an unusual problem recently.
Wife: She didn't say it had to be an unusual problem.
Husband: The question said something about being recent.
Wife: It's close enough.
Husband: It's close enough? Okay. Go ahead. Discuss.
Wife: How about that you won't ever discuss things with me? You make me discuss them by myself.
Husband: Has that been bothering you recently?
Wife: No.
Husband: I didn't think so.

The couple then go through a few other issues, but decide that each of these is not appropriate, either. At the end, the wife commented somewhat disappointedly, "I thought maybe we could have something to disagree about." In their intimacy interviews, the issues of separate interests, not having enough time together, and the fact that they do not talk much all were mentioned. The problem-solving excerpt makes clear that the couple gave fairly accurate descriptions of their situation in their individual interviews. In this case, they have "accommodated" to a reality of their marriage, but this accommodation has not been translated into improved communication. Similarly, the spouses in another couple both mentioned mutual accommodation as an important feature of their relationship, one that they felt they had experienced. During the problem-solving task, though, they were literally counting the minutes because they could think of nothing to say. At the end of a rather bland discussion of some minor problems involving their children, they called out together to the interviewer, "Help. . .we're stuck!"

Taken as a whole, the couples married longer than 10 years with low communication scores demonstrated a number of the same difficulties as the younger couples with similar communication scores. In addition, it appeared as though the more destructive type of couples had sharpened their modes of attack, escalation, and criticism so as to compete more effectively with each other for dominance of the situation. The tendency to avoid conflict noted in some of the poorly communicating shorter-married couples seemed to have become transformed into a communication gap so broad that the couple could not even occupy five minutes of time with a conversation about their problems.

Couples with High Communication Scores

These couples, like their younger counterparts, were supportive, helpful and nondefensive toward each other as they shared their common concerns about their relationship. One of the themes that preoccupied these couples was the lack of time they had to spend with each other. The first couple in this group dealt at length with some possible solutions to this mutual problem:

Husband: Do you have anything?
Wife: The only thing I can think of is the fact that it's the same old thing.
Husband: What's that?
Wife: Never, we just don't. . .I still feel a lot of times, and I guess maybe it's just all the overtime, that I don't get to talk to you. Don't you feel that? I mean we're together and we're doing things. . .(but) we don't get to talk to each other.
Husband: Right. I agree.
Wife: (laughs).
Husband: We don't spend enough, we still don't spend enough time

together, 'cause we don't seem to have enough time with all the other,

Wife: And I don't see that that's a thing that we can change right now. Really.

Husband: No, uh, we don't schedule enough time together. I mean we go but we go out bowling or we go out to a movie and,

Wife: We should just go out by ourselves.

Husband: Yeah, or maybe we should just go and have dinner or something, right?

Wife: Yeah. I really enjoy that. 'Cause we actually sit there and talk to each other (laughs). That's why I've been kind of not looking forward to the party at Pete and Joan's on Saturday night.

Husband: Right, because it's another

Wife: Lots of people

Husband: night out where we'll be with lots of other people, so although we're together

Wife: Right.

Husband: We don't have a long period of time where we can sit down and talk.

Wife: Right. And then the following week we're supposed to be going out with Mike, Sally, John, and Betsy.

Husband: For our anniversary.

Wife: Yeah, I'd rather just go out with you.

Husband: Okay, well let's do that next week. We'll just go out.

Wife: We can't, though. We've made the reservations.

Husband: Oh, we're already going

Wife: We've planned on it for ages, you know.

Husband: We're already going out to a concert next Wednesday.

Wife: Right.

Husband: So, we're going out next Wednesday and we're going out next Saturday. Well, what we could do,

Wife: What we could do is to make a date to go out with each other, not anybody else.

Husband: Right.

Wife: And I think that's what happens, when you go to those big parties. Pete and Joan say you and I always talk to each other at their parties. When it's a party of that size, it's almost like you are on your own. I mean, you're all by yourself, you might as well be, because you can't talk to all those people. It's too noisy.

Husband: Right. That's right. I enjoy just going there to see what the party's like, who's going to be there, what kind of people, and you know, just kind of hanging around and having a drink and talking to you is fine with me.

Wife: I know what else I want to ask you, though. Now that we agree

Husband: we've got to make a date, just go out, you and me. Right?
Husband: Right.

Their discussion of this issue has led to no change in the couple's intentions, but it has allowed them to redefine their problem in such a way that it provides a sort of resolution to their difficulty. Both partners had, it might be pointed out, complained in the intimacy interview about the lack of opportunity they have to spend time together. In her words: "It seems to me like we talked about more important things before we got married than after we got married." From her husband's perspective:

It's so easy to get caught up in spending the time doing other things. We have to schedule time to spend with each other and if you don't do that, it's easy for the relationship to deteriorate.

There is a concordance, then, between the spouse identities of this couple and the content of their dialogue. Both see themselves as losing touch with each other due to the pressure of outside commitments. What they may not be as ready to observe, however, is the discrepancy between their stated desires to see each other more, and their behavior, which keeps them from finding more intense ways to interact. Both partners share the myth that it is all their "outside commitments" that prevent them from finding time to be together. They do not see that their outside commitments are a matter of choice. This couple's predicament provides a good example of the discrepancies that can occur between mutual accommodation of identities within the relationship and the "objective reality" of the couple's existence. They both share the same distorted picture of the factors that stand in the way of their ability to spend more time together.

Other couples in this group chose to devote their problem-solving session to finding ways to spend more time together, but similarly were unable to achieve any resolution. The common theme that permeated the dialogues of these couples was that they wished to see each other more, but there were unavoidable forces that impeded their realizing this wish. They had, then, accommodated their identities to this "fact" of life, but were unaware of how discrepant this accommodation was from the possibilities that lay before them. Although the way they communicated their concerns was positive, supportive, and nondefensive, they both failed to address the underlying problem. Furthermore, as the preceding excerpt shows, they were not actually willing to make any sincere effort to change the situation. As one couple put it, after a lengthy discussion of ways that they might socialize more together:

Husband: I think you're dreaming, but that's all right.
Wife: I know I'm dreaming, but I'd like it anyway.

The mutual accommodation process, to the extent that it involves the creation of a joint "dream," can therefore have its drawbacks.

This analysis of the communication task has provided a kind of anchoring point to the examination of the intimacy interviews similar to that discussed by Levinger (1977). We can see, in these excerpts, the dynamics of how the two spouse identities of the partners interact in ways not possible to observe with the individual interviews. More importantly, we have also seen that the identity processes can take two forms: one, involving the relationship of the spouses to each other; the second involving the relationship between the mutual identity of the spouses and the "reality" of the outside observer's point of view.

8
Summary and Conclusions

We have now seen what the husbands and wives in our sample have had to say about their views of themselves and each other in their relationships. We have also had the opportunity to observe their interactions while involved in the process of trying to resolve a problem. It is now time to summarize these observations and examine their implications for the understanding of identity and intimacy in marriage.

It is apparent that the concept of "spouse identity" is a very real one to the individuals in these couples. The answers they gave concerning their impressions of various features of their relationship reflected, in part, their impressions of their partners and the nature of their relationship. More, if not equally, important, the responses to the questions from the intimacy interview also reflected their expectations, desires, ideals, values, and attitudes about being a spouse. Furthermore, the responses to the intimacy interview reflected more than simple attempts made by spouses to "look good" in comparison to their partners, or in comparison to other married people. The responses given by the individuals in the sample to the intimacy interview questions were influenced by their views of the self that make up their identities as married people.

These spouse identities were, as the analyses in this book showed, vital and dynamic. This is particularly true given that the identity of one spouse is constantly in interaction with the identity of the partner. The effects the two individuals exert on each other are reciprocal, and the direction of influence is constantly shifting. It is for these reasons that it is difficult to isolate or trace the causal sequence of identity processes. Furthermore, the identities of the partners interact within the context of some sort of "objective" reality of their relationship. The outside observer sees the interaction of the two spouses and forms impressions that may, and probably do, deviate sharply from the views of the spouses within the relationship.

The problem of evaluating the identity processes against "objective" criteria has been a constant issue in the present study. Many times we have been forced to speculate on who was "right," or if not right, who was accommodating to whom and who was assimilating their identity onto their responses. The main point was, as we continued to emphasize, not whether it was the husband or the wife who was assimilating or accommodating, but what the spouses believed to be the case about the nature of their effects on each other. The only places in which firmer conclusions could be reached about the identity processes was when there was a relatively objective piece of information, such as the dialogue from the communication excerpt or an inference made possible by the accumulated evidence.

Given these inevitable problems involved in analyzing data as complex as these, there are a number of conclusions we feel confident in making about the nature of adult identity in the intimate relationship. Some of these conclusions will seem familiar to the student of marriage and the family; we do not claim originality for these. The perspective we do hope to add to these well-known findings is offered by the focus in this study on identity and how it influences marital interaction. Furthermore, it is the nature of identity to change, grow, and differentiate, as well as to provide the adult with a sense of continuity over time. By adopting the developmental perspective implied in the concept of identity, we also hope to highlight the dynamic and ever-changing nature of intimate relationships.

Identity and Its Relation to Marital Adjustment in Husbands and Wives

The identities of husbands and wives differed in a number of important ways. We are reluctant to attribute these differences to gender per se, but see them as a function of the historical time period in which these people are living. These couples were formed at a time of transition in cultural ideals of marriage. Expectations about how wives and husbands should behave in the marital interaction were shifting and are continuing to evolve. On the one hand, the members of the sample were raised in a time when traditional views of masculinity and femininity prevailed. Countering this, the couples were married at a time when the concept of equality between the sexes had just taken hold. As a result, the spouse identities of these people contain mixed expectations that at times can create confusion for them and ambiguity in their relationship. Whatever the cause, however, we want to emphasize here that when we discuss gender differences, we are focusing on divergence rather than commonalities. There were exceptions within the husband and wife groups to the general statements we are making here. Our analysis focuses on differences for the purpose of learning from the contrasts, for these stand out in sharper relief than the similarities.

First, then, husbands and wives differed considerably in the content of their identities. Wives regarded themselves as partners in egalitarian relationships, with a great deal of togetherness and sharing. As part of their own spouse identities, wives formulated an image of their husbands that enhanced this perception. They saw their husbands as interested in them, willing to help at all times, and desirous of as close and mutual an emotional bond as possible. Wives also regarded it as important that power be shared and that no one person in the relationship assume a dominant role overall. If the wife had more decision-making control over minor areas of the couple's life, it was important for her to see that as balanced by the husband's greater or at least equal authority in the category of major practical decisions. So far, then, the spouse identities of wives was based on egalitarian principles. Imbalance emerged, however, when it came to the question of who was expected to initiate sexual relationships. The wives clearly felt that it was the husband's job to pursue them. Furthermore, wives expected husbands to read their signals that they were in a pursuable state. This incongruity between the overall identities of the wives as egalitarian partners and their identities as sexual partners is one that most wives do not experience as problematic. For many of their husbands, though, it is a source of constant confusion and even annoyance. At the same time, however, husbands encourage or at least do not challenge the behavior of their wives.

We now come to the essence of the spouse identities of husbands. Like their wives, they share in egalitarian principles about marriage. They prefer to view themselves on an equal footing with their wives. Furthermore, the husband's identity is that he is a good lover who is able to satisfy his wife sexually and emotionally. The husband's spouse identity has its own special incongruity, however. This is his view of himself as the romantic hero, who is able to be an ideal husband but also has challenges of his own to pursue. As much as he loves his wife and wants to spend time with her, he also has independent needs to fulfill. These needs include the pursuit of his career, but are also oriented to his development as an individual outside the relationship. The bind the husband therefore creates is that he sets up expectations for his wife toward which he himself feels ambivalent. Should his wife let him pursue his independent goals, he will worry that she does not care about him. Should his wife take his desire for mutuality at face value, he will feel that his hands have been tied. In either case, there is a potential for misunderstanding and unhappiness.

The nature of the identity processes also differs considerably between husbands and wives. A wife uses assimilation to fit her image of her husband into her own spouse identity as a partner in an egalitarian relationship. A husband attempts to assimilate his perceptions of himself into his own spouse identity as a loving and romantic mate. He views his wife mainly in terms of her general abilities to enhance his identity. Neither husbands nor wives, then, see their partners very accurately. However, they differ in the nature of their inaccuracies. The wife notices the particular characteristics of her husband in much more detail, even as she transforms her perceptions of these characteristics into ones that match her identity as a spouse in an egalitarian relationship. The husband pays little attention to the personal qualities of his wife as an individual. Instead, he sees her for what she represents: a stabilizing influence who meets his domestic needs. Through his relationship with her, he can progress in his development as an individual. The husband's assimilation differs from the wife's, then, in the direction toward which it is targeted. He directs assimilation toward his view of himself in the relationship, not toward his view of his wife.

This is a major difference, then, between the identity processes used by husbands and wives. The wife directs her assimilation toward her husband, the husband toward himself. The husband is, for both partners, the object of greater assimilative efforts.

Consistent with these differences in the identity processes, it is the husband's qualities as an intimate partner that set the pace for the marital interactions. The husband's potential to be intimate was found to have a greater role in determining the marital adjustment of his wife than was the intimacy of the wife in influencing the marital adjustment of her husband. Thus, it is true that a wife will attempt to assimilate her view of her husband into her identity as a spouse in an egalitarian and close relationship. This process is made much easier, however, and is more successful if the husband truly is oriented toward closeness and egalitarianism. The wife has less assimilating to do, and at the same time, may learn from her husband about how she can be more intimate herself. Again, though, the highly intimate husband places himself in a difficult position when he "teaches" his wife to be more intimate. Naturally, she will come to demand and expect that her husband match her commitment to having an equitable and close relationship. Her husband will find it difficult to extricate himself from this situation, and he may try to find ways to ensure greater privacy for himself. He must keep his wife from finding out about these desires of his, though, or the process will be set into reverse.

It is the development over time of the processes set in motion in the younger couples about which we can only speculate from the data on the couples whose marriage has lasted from 11 to 20 years. We will turn next to the tentative conclusions that we were able to reach on the basis of the cross-sectional comparisons made between these two groups of couples.

Identity Processes in Couples According to Length of Marriage

The ability to compromise was seen by husbands and wives as the key factor leading to the success of a marriage among the couples in the longer-married group. Assimilation of one's partner to one's own identity as a spouse was a feature far more characteristic of the wives married 10 years or less. In the longer-married group, adaptation to the spouse's qualities entered as a predictor of marital adjustment, at least for wives. Thus, in terms of both the conscious experiences of couples and the data analyses, accommodation became far more of a crucial feature of the well-adjusted enduring marriage.

As the analysis of transcript excerpts showed, there are two types of accommodation within a marriage. One is the adjustment of partners to each other as each learns to incorporate features of the spouse identity of the partner into their own identities. The second type of accommodation is the recognition of "objective" qualities of the marriage. For example, a couple might recognize that they are not communicating as well as they could. The spouses may also attest to differences not previously acknowledged in their interests, personal styles, and values. It may also become apparent to the spouses that they have a limited ability to achieve the "perfect" relationship, because each of them has difficulty in being completely intimate. As it turned out, when couples talked about "compromise," they were referring to a relative form of adaptation made to each other's version of "reality" rather than to the externally validated qualities of the relationship, such as the intimacy potential of the partners or how well they communicated with each other.

The consequences of mutual accommodation, then, were not to help the couple adapt to the circumstances in which they found themselves, but to have the couple adopt an increasingly similar view of themselves and their relationship. When we examined the transcripts of the intimacy interviews, we suspected that this situation might be occurring, and that over time couples could become further removed from the "true" nature of their relationship. It was not until we examined the communication excerpts, with the outside perspective that these made possible, that it became evident that this process was in fact occurring. Couples had accommodated to myths about their relationship rather than to features that an outside observer would find strikingly apparent. It was the consonance on these myths, such as "We don't have enough time together," that seemed to have resulted from their mutual accommodation to each other's perceptions of the relationship. The obvious danger of this kind of accommodation is that couples lose sight of the problems in their relationship that threaten to undermine the very harmony that they think they have achieved. What may be particularly damaging to the relationship is the lack of preparation the spouses have for accommodating to the problem when for some reason it can no longer be avoided by the members of the couple. A couple whose communication is at a high level and who think that they have their difficulties under control would be especially demoralized when they find that their relationship is atrophying because they do not make enough time for each other in their daily schedules. This is particularly so because the issue of dependence and independence within the relationship is highly loaded with the potential for misperceptions and conflict between husbands and wives.

Compromise to "what" then becomes the key question when discussing the identities of couples in long-term relationships. Couple who adapt to each other gain the advantage of incorporating in increasingly larger doses the spouse identities of their partners. They run the risk, however, of losing sight of the direction in which their relationship is headed.

Conclusion: Identity Processes in Intimacy

This study of married couples has highlighted a number of significant ways in which the identities of adults as spouses interact with the quality of the intimate relationship between them. Clearly, this investigation would not have been possible without the availability of responses of both partners in the relationship. Given the many disparities between husbands and wives in their responses to the intimacy interview, it is clear that the prevailing practice of evaluating a person's intimacy on the sole basis of an individual interview cannot be considered a valid one. Furthermore, it has become apparent that much can be learned about the individuals and their relationship by comparing areas of agreement and disagreement between them in their responses to the interview questions.

Apart from this methodological insight, the present study has brought fundamental husband-wife differences in spouse identities into sharp relief. Husbands and wives define themselves as spouses according to divergent standards, many of which follow traditional masculine and feminine sex-role stereotypes. Other gender differences in spouse identities reflect attempts by both partners to adopt to more contemporary views of marriage as a collaboration among equals. Husbands and wives forge very different integrations of these disparate sets of ideals and values, and these differences form the basis for serious potential misunderstandings. The problems are in many ways exacerbated by the false sense of security and complacency that the better-communicating and more well-adjusted couples develop over their years together. They see their relationship persisting where others have failed, and so attribute a magical degree of success to their own marriages. However, blinded by a mutual accommodation to each other's spouse identities, these couples fail to see the fault lines in their relationship.

There are, despite these gloomy assessments, many ways in which couples can grow as individuals and as a pair through the operation of the identity processes. We have seen wives report becoming better able to communicate and resolve problems through the interventions of their husbands. Similarly, the attempt that couples make to accommodate to each other has its benefits as the alliance between them is strengthened and solidified. It is important to recall, as we recognize these features of the marriages studied here, Erikson's writings about intimacy. The ability to relate closely to another adult is enhanced by the strength of one's identity. The relationship between identity and intimacy is, however, reciprocal. Perhaps the greatest impetus for growth of identity is through the unique and intense bond that the intimate relationship can offer.

Practical Implications

Our goal in writing this book was to contribute to the research literature on intimacy in marriage; there are, in addition, several practical implications of the findings. First, it is clear that the view presented by one partner in a relationship is unlikely to be an accurate representation. Therapy or counseling in which an individual's close relationships become an issue must, therefore, take into account the perspective of that individual's partner. Although this concept is widely accepted and forms the basis for a couple's approach to treatment of relationship difficulties, it might not be recognized as important in the treatment of individuals. As we have shown in this book, the individual is quite likely to present a view of the close relationship that is influenced by that individual's identity within the relationship.

The second practical implication of our research concerns the nature of the mutual accommodation process. We have shown that, over time, couples adopt identities of themselves in the relationship that often do not correspond to the reality of their interaction. Couples who accommodate relative to each other run the risk of losing sight of the true nature of their relationship. In the process, they create a void that becomes more and more difficult to bridge because they lose the ability and motivation to communicate with each other. It would seem that the only way to avoid this dilemma is for couples to have pointed out to both of them the discrepancy between their mutually arrived-at identities and the more objective features of their joint experiences. At the same time, it is important to respect the healthy accommodations that couples make to each other over time and to encourage this process to continue. Crucial to the success of these developments, as this study has shown, is a context of clear and frequent communication.

The willingness to set aside traditional masculine and feminine stereotypes is another crucial factor in the fostering of intimacy over the course of marriage. Couples who hold stereotyped beliefs concerning the roles of men and women in marriage are at a great disadvantage when it comes to taking the perspective of the partner in the relationship. Furthermore, as this study has shown, sex-role stereotypes operate in very subtle ways so that even couples who believe themselves to be truly egalitarian relate to each other in ways that reinforce the gap between the genders. From a practical standpoint, it would seem important to determine the extent to which the spouse identities of couples are based on these beliefs. Whether these long-held beliefs can be corrected is a separate issue; however, it is likely that the couple would benefit from making explicit their biases regarding the roles of men and women in relationships.

In conclusion, the analyses presented in this book are intended to serve as models for the researcher or clinician to adopt in the assessment of individuals within relationships. It is only through careful attention to nuances of wording, discrepancies, and omissions, as was used in the analyses of the transcript excerpts, that identity processes can be traced and their patterns discerned. Apart from the conclusions reached in this study, we believe that this analytical process is one that can be useful in the treatment of marital problems and individual adjustment difficulties as well as research on the development of intimacy in relationships.

Appendix A
Questions on the Adult Intimacy Interview

1. How much free time do you spend together?
2a. What sort of things do you do to be together?
2b. How do these activities get planned?
3. What sort of things do you do to help your partner when he or she has a lot of work or is very busy?
4a. Do you feel you could rely on your spouse to help you if you needed it?
4b. Do you think your spouse feels s/he can rely on you?
5. When it comes to practical decisions regarding household chores or duties, do you discuss most things or do you make decisions independently of each other?
6. When planning recreational or leisure activities, do you discuss them with each other, or do you make independent decisions?
7. When making decisions regarding finances and expenditures, do you discuss most things or do you make independent decisions?
8. When making any career decisions, do you discuss them with each other, or do you make your own decisions?
9. Does one of you assume most of the responsibility for making major family decisions?
10. Does one of you assume most of the responsibility for making the everyday decisions?
11. Would you say that both of you can pursue your work-related goals or has one of you subordinated them to those of the other?
12. In the practical aspects of your relationship (leisure/recreation, household chores, money), would you say that one partner's wishes take precedence over those of the other, or would you say your wishes are followed equally?
13. How important is your relationship right now in comparison to other aspects of your life?
14a. How would you describe your feelings for your partner?
14b. How do you think your partner feels about you?
15. How important to you is it that your relationship lasts?

16. How much time do you spend thinking about your relationship?
17. How much do you and your partner talk about your feelings for each other?
18. Do you share your worries and problems with your partner?
19. Are there many things you couldn't or wouldn't share with your partner?
20. Do you feel free to say something critical to your partner?
21. When you and your partner disagree on some matter or just get on each other's nerves, how do you usually handle it?
22a. Do you ever fight or argue?
22b. When you fight or argue, are there any particular themes that it revolves around?
22c. What do you see as the main problems the two of you have to work out as a couple?
23a. What friendships do you pursue separately from each other?
23b. How do you feel about having separate friendships?
24a. What interests do you pursue separately from each other? (include all interests, both his and hers, as mentioned by the respondent)
24b. How do you two feel about your separate interests?
25a. What do you think your life would be like if you were not with your partner any longer?
25b. How do you think he/she would feel?
26. How do you feel if your partner makes a personal decision important to him/her without consulting you?
27a. How important to you is the sexual aspect of your relationship?
27b. How important do you think it is to your partner?
28a. Do you feel that your sexual activity is just routine, or is it exciting, or a combination of both?
28b. How do you think your partner feels?
29a. Do you ever hold back your sexual interest because of uncomfortable feelings toward your partner?
29b. Does your partner do this?
30a. Are you satisfied with the sex in your relationship?
30b. Do you think your partner is satisfied with the sex in your relationship?
31a. Are you physically affectionate and expressive?
31b. Is your partner physically affectionate and expressive?
32a. How difficult or easy is it for you to tell/ask your partner when you would like to have sex with him/her?
32b. How difficult or easy do you think it is for your partner?
33a. How easy or difficult is it for you to refuse your partner when she/he wants to initiate sex?
33b. How easy or difficult do you think it is for your partner?

34a.   How easy or difficult is it for you to talk to your partner about what you like or dislike about sex?

34b.   How comfortable does your partner seem when you talk about sex?

35.   Does one of you tend to initiate sexual activity more than the other?

36.   Who usually determines when you stop sexual activity?

37a.   Do you know if your partner has any preferences with regard to sex?

37b.   Do you usually try to go along with his/her preferences?

37c.   Is your partner aware of any preferences you might have?

37d.   Does he/she try to accommodate them?

38.   Do you feel sex is equal important to both of you or is it more important to one of you than the other?

39a.   What does a close or good relationship consist of as you see it?

39b.   How much have you attained?

Appendix B
Coding of Adult Intimacy Interview

1. How much free time do you spend together?
   Definition of free time: When neither of them are working. Does not include time doing household chores. This time must be spent with both in the same place (e.g., the same room of the house). This time can be spent playing with, talking to, or sharing in entertainment with the children.

   [A] *All free time*—means that they actually say they spend all their free time together. This does not qualify if they state any regular activities that they do not participate in together. Allow for about 1/2 hour per day of separation during the free time. If a percentage of free time is given, it must be 85% or more to be called "all free time." This category means all free time, not just a whole day or weekend.

   [B] *Most of their free time*—If they state that they spend most of their free time together. May have a couple of separate regular activities, but they must *state* more activities that they do together than they do not. Percentage-wise should be anywhere from 70 to 84%. It could also be thought as 2 hours a day plus one full weekend day.

   [C] *Average*—This can be considered 50 to 69% of their free time, or 30 minutes to an hour a day, with a day of the weekend spent together. Could be classified if they have a regularly occurring event that they both participate in. This also qualifies if they don't have much time during the week, but spend a good portion of the weekend together.

   [D] *Some time together*—Less than a half-hour every day, and half-day of weekend can be considered 20 to 49% of their free time together. This qualifies if all their free time consists of chores or errands.

   [E] *Almost none*—No regularly mutually participating events. No time spent together during the week, along with work-filled weekends. This classifies if they wait for vacations to be together. This can also be considered if they spend less than one day together every two weeks.

2a. What sort of things do you do to be together?
[A] Movies
[B] Dancing
[C] Dinner/lunch
[D] Visit friends
[E] Watch TV
[F] Read together
[G] Camping/hiking
[H] Fishing
[I] Household chores
[J] Work
[K] Child care
[L] Swimming/water sports
[M] Skiing·
[N] Tennis/racquetball
[O] Go to gym/spa
[P] Biking
[Q] Jogging
[R] Go to church/temple
[S] Shopping (recreational)
[T] Other

2b. How do these activities get planned?
[A] Both plan
[B] Husband
[C] Wife
[D] Mutual, but husband plans more often
[E] Mutual, but wife plans more often
[F] No plans: Instantaneous decision

3. What sort of things do you do to help your partner when he/she has a lot of work or is very busy?
[A] Anything they need help with
[B] Stay out of the way—keep quiet, not talk
[C] Housework, grocery shopping, errands
[D] Emotional support—just listening
[E] Taking charge of the children
[F] Nothing

4a. Do you feel you could rely on your spouse to help you if you needed it?
[A] Yes
[B] No
[C] Sometimes
[D] Usually

4b. Do you think your spouse feels s/he can rely on you?
   [A] Yes
   [B] No
   [C] Sometimes
   [D] Usually
5. When it comes to practical decisions regarding household chores or duties, do you discuss most things or do you make decisions independently of each other?
   (The following categories are used for Question 5 through 8)
   [A] No discussion; always independent decisions
   [B] Occasional discussion; mostly independent decisions
   [C] 1/2 discussion; 1/2 independent decisions
   [D] Mostly discussion; occasionally independent decisions
   [E] Always discussion; no independent decision
   [F] Used to discuss it; don't need to now
6. When planning recreational or leisure activities, do you discuss them with each other, or do you make independent decisions?
7. When making decisions regarding finances and expenditures, do you discuss most things or do you make independent decisions?
8. When making any career decisions, do you discuss them with each other, or do you make your own decisions?
9. Does one of you assume most of the responsibility for making major family decisions?
   [A] Yes—Husband
   [B] Yes—Wife
   [C] No—Both
10. Does one of you assume most of the responsibility for making the everyday decisions?
   [A] Yes—Husband
   [B] Yes—Wife
   [C] No—Both
   [D] It depends
11. Would you say that both of you can pursue your work-related goals or has one of you subordinated them to those of the other?
   [A] Both can pursue their work goals/no subordination.
   [B] One has subordinated his/her goals.
      [1] Wife's goals are subordinated
      [2] Husband's goals are subordinated

   * Subordination is not considered to be raising children instead of working, when the childraiser wants that for his or her goal.

12. In the practical aspects of your relationship (leisure/recreation, household chores, money), would you say that one partner's wishes take precedence over those of the other, or would you say your wishes are followed equally?

[A]   Equally
[B]   Wife's wishes take precedence.
[C]   Husband's wishes take precedence.
[D]   Most of the time there is equality, but the husband's wishes have occasion to take precedence.
[E]   Most of the time there is equality, but the wife's wishes have occasion to take precedence.

13.   How important is your relationship right now in comparison to other aspects of your life?
[A]   Most important—#1, more important than anything else, central to everything, more important than career, very important.
[B]   Important—a steadying influence, 80%, establishes overtones for other things
[C]   Fairly important—equal to other things, such as career
[D]   Not that important—wouldn't go to all lengths to keep it, other things are more important

14a.   How would you describe your feelings for your partner?

(These ratings are also used for Question 14b.)
[A]   Supportive
[B]   Warm
[C]   Easygoing
[D]   Close
[E]   Respectful
[F]   Loving
[G]   Caring
[H]   Couldn't replace them (they're part of my life)
[I]   Best friend
[J]   Trusting
[K]   Other (specify)

14b.   How do you think your partner feels about you?

15.   How important to you is it that your relationship lasts?
[A]   Most important, #1, central, very important
[B]   Fairly important, cyclical (not specifically stated as most important thing or qualified in some way)
[C]   Not that important

16.   How much time do you spend thinking about your relationship?
[A]   A lot—daily; it's always there.
[B]   A significant amount of time—frequently, quite a bit
[C]   Moderately
[D]   Not much—take it for granted, 10% or less
[E]   Cyclically—when there is a specific problem
[F]   None

17.   How much do you and your partner talk about your feelings for each other?

[A]   Often; a great deal
[B]   Occasionally; once in a while
[C]   Not much; not enough
[D]   Never
[E]   Not much but enough

18.   Do you share your worries and problems with your partner?
[A]   Yes, definitely
[B]   Most of the time
[C]   Sometimes
[D]   Yes, except when I know my partner won't want to deal with it.
[E]   No

19.   Are there many things you couldn't or wouldn't share with your partner?
[A]   Yes, money
[B]   Yes, about things she/he has no interest in
[C]   Yes, about work
[D]   Yes, about children
[E]   Yes, if my partner is stressed
[F]   Yes, but very few
[G]   No, nothing I wouldn't share
[H]   Yes (in general)

20.   Do you feel free to say something critical to your partner?
[A]   Yes (may be concerned about how it is worded but does not feel restricted in terms of content).
[B]   Sometimes, but have to be careful of what it's about.
[C]   No.

21.   When you and your partner disagree on some matter or just get on each other's nerves, how do you usually handle it?
[A]   Fight
[B]   Yell/scream
[C]   Talk/discuss it
[D]   Wife gives in to husband
[E]   Husband gives in to wife
[F]   Walk away from each other (drop it, go to bed, etc.)
[G]   Engage in another activity (reading, watch TV, etc.)
[H]   Other (specify)

22a. Do you ever fight or argue?
[A]   Yes,   [1]   Frequently
              [2]   Occasionally
              [3]   Rarely
[B]   No
[C]   No fights, we disagree

22b. When you fight or argue, are there any particular themes that it revolves around?

(These ratings are also used for Question 22c.)
[A] Balancing of priorities
[B] Backgrounds—family
[C] Money
[D] Communication
[E] Household things
[F] Children—including the fact that we have children
[G] Small things
[H] Work—job-related problems
[I] Different goals or philosophies of life
[J] Being more understanding
[K] Moodiness
[L] Sex
[M] Don't fight
[N] Other

22c.   What do you see as the main problems the two of you have to work out as a couple?

23a.   What friendships do you pursue separately from each other?

(Questions 23 and 24 are rated on two dimensions)
Ratings for agreement about relationship:
[A] Friends are mostly separate (for one or both).
[B] Friends are mostly mutual to the couple; some friends outside but these are not important.
[C] Neither have separate friendships at all.
Ratings for self-intimacy:
[A] Have no separate friends but spouse does.
[B] Have separate friends but spouse does not.
[C] Have mostly mutual friends that have evolved over the marriage.
[D] Both have mostly separate friends that each has cultivated on his or her own.
[E] Spouse has gotten to know my friends (this incorporates category B above).
[F] I have gotten to know spouse's friends (this incorporates category A above).

23b.   How do you feel about having separate friendships?
[A] Present situation is fine.
[B] Present situation has problems.

24a.   What interests do you pursue separately from each other? (include all interests, both his and hers, as mentioned by the respondent)
Ratings for agreement about relationship:
[A] Athletic interests
[B] Political activities

[C]   Reading
[D]   Playing an instrument
[E]   Hobbies
[F]   Clubs
[G]   Art
[H]   Computers (work doesn't count)
[I]   Concerts (music)
[J]   Shopping (for fun)
[K]   None (since marriage)
[L]   House projects
[M]   Work
[N]   Automobiles, motorcycles
[O]   Movies
[P]   Other (specify)
Ratings for co-determination:
[A]   Have no separate interests but spouse does.
[B]   Have separate interests but spouse does not.
[C]   Have mostly mutual interests that evolved together.
[D]   Both have mostly separate interests that have evolved independently.
[E]   Spouse has gotten interested in what I do.
[F]   I have gotten interested in what spouse does.

24b.   How do you two feel about your separate interests?
[A]   Positive
[B]   Negative
[C]   Fine, as long as they don't take up too much time

25a.   What do you think your life would be like if you were not with your partner any longer?

(These ratings are also used for Question 25b.)
[A]   Would be devastated, very distraught or distressed.
[B]   Unhappy, but would manage; quality of life reduced greatly; would have to make changes in life style that would be emotionally difficult but manageable.
[C]   Would be temporarily put out but would carry on with not too much difficulty thereafter; practical problems are more of a concern than emotional (no mention of unhappiness).
[D]   Would be better off alone or with another spouse.

25b.   How do you think he/she would feel?

26.   How do you feel if your partner makes a personal decision important to him/her without consulting you?
[A]   No problem under any circumstances; spouses should be able to make separate decisions.
[B]   It is okay as long as it doesn't affect me or the family; if it does affect me directly then I do get irritated.

[C]   Disappointed or hurt, feel left out.
[D]   Don't or wouldn't like it, get angry or aggravated *even if it does not directly affect me.*
[E]   It doesn't happen because almost all our decisions are jointly made.

27a.   How important to you is the sexual aspect of your relationship?
[A]   Very important
[B]   Somewhat or pretty important, but not the most by any means.
[C]   Not that important
[D]   Cyclical

27b.   How important do you think it is to your partner?
[A]   Very important
[B]   Somewhat or pretty important, but not the most by any means
[C]   Not that important
[D]   Cyclical
[E]   Don't know
[F]   More important than to me
[G]   Less important than to me
[H]   The same as it is to me

28a.   Do you feel that your sexual activity is just routine, or is it exciting, or a combination of both?

(These ratings are also used for Question 28b.)
[A]   Routine
[B]   Sometimes routine, sometimes exciting
[C]   Neither one nor the other
[D]   Exciting

28b.   How do you think your partner feels?

29a.   Do you ever hold back your sexual interest because of uncomfortable feelings toward your partner?

(These ratings are also used for Question 29b.)
[A]   No
[B]   Rarely; once in awhile; not too often
[C]   Occasionally, at times
[D]   Yes, more than occasionally

29b.   Does your partner do this?

30a.   Are you satisfied with the sex in your relationship?
[A]   Yes
[B]   Somewhat, sometimes, more or less.
[C]   No

30b.   Do you think your partner is satisfied with the sex in your relationship?
[A]   Yes
[B]   Somewhat, sometimes, more or less
[C]   No

      [D]   I hope so, I think so
      [E]   Not sure; I don't know

31a. Are you physically affectionate and expressive?

      (These ratings are also used for Question 31b.)
      [A]   Yes
      [B]   Sometimes
      [C]   Not too often
      [D]   No

31b. Is your partner physically affectionate and expressive?

32a. How difficult or easy is it for you to tell/ask your partner when you would like to have sex with him/her?

      (These ratings are used for Questions 32 through 34.)
      [A]   Easy.
      [B]   Sometimes easy, sometimes difficult.
      [C]   Difficult (or never does).

32b. How difficult or easy do you think it is for your partner?

33a. How easy or difficult is it for you to refuse your partner when she/he wants to initiate sex?

33b. How easy or difficult do you think it is for your partner?

34a. How easy or difficult is it for you to talk to your partner about what you like or dislike about sex?

34b. How comfortable does your partner seem when you talk about sex?

35.   Does one of you tend to initiate sexual activity more than the other?

      (These ratings are also used for Question 36.)
      [A]   Husband does
      [B]   Wife does
      [C]   Mutual
      [D]   Sometimes one, sometimes the other
      [E]   Yes, unspecified who does

36.   Who usually determines when you stop sexual activity?

37a. Do you know if your partner has any preferences with regard to sex?
      [A]   Yes
      [B]   No

37b. Do you usually try to go along with his/her preferences?
      [A]   Yes
      [B]   Most times
      [C]   Sometimes
      [D]   Once in a while (occasionally)
      [E]   Never

37c. Is your partner aware of any preferences you might have?
      [A]   Yes
      [B]   No
      [C]   I don't know

37d. Does he/she try to accommodate them?
   [A]   Yes
   [B]   Most times
   [C]   Sometimes
   [D]   Once in a while (occasionally)
   [E]   Never
38. Do you feel sex is equally important to both of you or is it more important to one of you than the other?
   [A]   Equally important
   [B]   More important to husband
   [C]   More important to wife
39a. What does a close or good relationship consist of as you see it?
   [A]   Individuality within the marriage
   [B]   Space
   [C]   Communication
   [D]   Honesty
   [E]   Agreement
   [F]   Division of labor
   [G]   Sex
   [H]   Enjoying one another's presence
   [I]   Respect
   [J]   Trust
   [K]   Compromise
   [L]   Laughter
   [M]   Friendship
   [N]   Mutual goals
   [O]   Support
   [P]   Touching
   [Q]   Commitment
   [R]   Love
   [S]   Other
39b. How much have you attained?
   [A]   100%
   [B]   A lot—most of it, very well
   [C]   Quite a bit—pretty good, some places need work
   [D]   It's cyclical
   [E]   Not much

Appendix C
Measures Derived from the Intimacy Interview

Ratings from the intimacy interview were consolidated into three composite measures representing the average of the husband's and wife's score for each couple.[1] The three measures represent each couple's accurate perceptions of each other and their relationship, their perceived similarity to each other concerning their feelings about the marriage, and potential as individuals to be intimate in a long-term relationship.

Accurate Perception

The accurate perception score is based on two components that represent how clearly the partners in the couple are perceiving each other and their relationship. The total accurate perception score is based on two sets of ratings: (1) the couple's agreement on questions about their relationship; and (2) how closely each spouse can predict what the partner will say in response to questions about the relationship.

Agreement scores were obtained by a system in which total agreement received the highest score, one category away from total agreement the next highest score, and so on. The following system was used for assigning agreement scores.

Question 1—How much free time:
(A = Total, E = None)
4 = complete agreement
3 = AB, BC, CD, DE
2 = AC, BD, CE

---

[1] Analyses conducted with separate husband and wife scores yielded comparable results; the average husband and wife score was used because it is a more stable measure.

1 = AD, BE
0 = AE

Question 2a—What they do in free time:
Numerator=   Number of activities in common
Denominator = Total number of different activities mentioned by H + W

Question 2b—How these activities get planned:
(A + F = Mutual; B + D = Husband; C + E = Wife)
2 = complete agreement
1 = AD, AE, AF, DF, EF, BD, CE
0 = AB, AC, BE, BF, CD, CF

Questions 5 through 8—Discussion of practical decisions (responses to these four questions were averaged before being added into the agreement score)
(A = 0 Discussion; E = 100% Discussion):
5 = complete agreement
4 = AB, BC, CD, DE, EF
3 = AC, BD, CE, DF
2 = AD, BE, CF
1 = AE, BF
0 = AF

Questions 9 + 10—Responsibility for family decisions:
(A = Husband, B = Wife, C + D = Mutual)
1 = complete agreement
0 = AB, AC, BC, AD, BD

Question 11—Pursuing work-related goals:
(A = No subordination; B1 = Wife, B2 = Husband)
1 = complete agreement (1 extra point for B1 − B1, B2 − B2 agreement)
0 = AB

Question 12—Whose wishes are followed:
(A = Equal; B + E = Wife; C + D = Husband)
2 = complete agreement
1 = AD, AE, CD, BE
0 = AB, AC, BC, DE, CE

Question 17—Talk about feelings:
(A = Often; C + E = Not much)
3 = complete agreement
2 = AB, BC, BE, CD, DE

1 = AC, AE, BD
0 = AD

Question 21—Handling disagreement:
Numerator =   Number of methods in common
Denominator = Total number of different methods mentioned by H + W

Question 22a—Whether they fight or argue:
2 = complete agreement (give one extra point for agreement on A1, A2,
    or A3).
1 = BC, AC
0 = AB

Questions 22b + c—Areas of disagreements and problems:
Numerator =   Number of areas in common
Denominator = Total number of areas mentioned (H + W combined)

Question 23a—Separate friends:
2 = complete agreement
1 = BC
0 = AC, AB

Question 24a—Separate interests:
Numerator =   Number of areas in common
Denominator = Total number of areas mentioned (H + W combined)

Questions 23b + 24b—How they feel about separate interests:
1 = complete agreement (including AC)
0 = AB, BC

Question 35 + 36—Who initiates and stops sexual activity:
(A = Husband, B = Wife, C + D = Mutual)
2 = complete agreement
1 = CD, AE, BE
0 = AB, AC, BC, CE

Question 38—Is sex equally important to both:
(A = Mutual; B = Husband; C = Wife)
1 = complete agreement
0 = AB, AC, BC

Question 39b—How much of a good relationship they have attained:
(A = 100%)
3 = complete agreement

2 = AB, BC, CD
1 = AC, BE, AD
0 = AE

Although initially placed into the "Self-intimacy" category, it became apparent in analyzing the responses to Questions 23, 24, and 26 (concerning independent friends, activities, and decisions) that these questions also could be used in the assessment of agreement. Each spouse was asked to give an independent appraisal of the mutuality of the relationship in responding to these questions. Given that these questions were structurally similar to the others in this category, it was deemed appropriate to score them for agreement independently of self-intimacy.

Accurate prediction scores were based on questions in which the spouses were asked to state how they thought their partners would respond to the same question. In many cases, both spouses gave identical responses when asked to state their own individual perception. When they were then asked to predict how their partners would respond, it was therefore not possible to determine whether the couple were perceiving each other accurately, or whether they were projecting their own response onto their partner. The only condition in which true accuracy could be measured was the case in which the partners gave different individual responses. When asked to predict the partner's response, the spouse would then be making an independent judgment. Consider the following example based on Question 14, "How do you feel about your spouse?" The husband states that he feels "respect" for his wife; the wife states that she feels that he is her "best friend." These responses would qualify for accuracy determination, because the husband and wife give different individual responses to the question. An "accurate" response by the husband would then be if he predicted that his wife feels that he is her best friend; an "inaccurate" response by the wife would be if she predicted that her husband would say that he feels that he can trust her.

The following questions were used to calculate "Accuracy": 3, 4, 14, 25, 27–34, and 37. On the basis of these questions, the number of responses that met the criteria for accurate perceptions were counted for each husband and wife. From this total was subtracted the number of inaccurate perceptions. The remainder was added to the "agreement" score to form the total "Accurate Perception" score.

Perceived Similarity

The extent to which couples perceive that they are similar to each other was calculated on the basis of the "Accuracy" questions in Appendix B. The perceived similarity scores had two components: (1) the number of times a spouse said that his or her partner felt the "same" (using this word in the response); and (2) the number of times the spouse predicted that the partner would give the same response as the spouse (for example, the husband says that he feels satisfied with the sex in their relationship, and predicts that the wife is also satisfied with the sex they have).

Self-Intimacy

The individual spouse's potential to be intimate within a close relationship was assessed by the "self-intimacy" questions listed below. These questions approximate Erikson's concept of intimacy as the ability to share the vulnerable aspects of one's self with a partner. The responses given to these questions are based on subjective assessments of the individual's own feelings. They were scored according to how closely these assessments fit the "ideal" of the intimate partner as described by Erikson's concept of intimacy. The following criteria were used for assigning scores.

Question 13—Importance of relationship:
A = 4, B = 3, C = 2, D = 1

Question 15—Importance of enduring:
A = 2, B = 1, C = 0

Question 16—Time spent thinking:
A = 5, B = 4, C = 3, D = 2, E = 1, F = 0

Question 17—Share worries and problems:
A = 4, B = 3, C = 2, D = 1, E = 0

Question 18—Things couldn't or wouldn't share:
G = 3, A–E = 2, F = 1, H = 0

Question 20—Feel free to criticize:
A = 2, B = 1, C = 0

Questions 23a + 24a—Friends and interests
B + E = Self dominant
C + D = No one dominant
A + F = Spouse dominant

Question 26—Separate decisions
A, B, E = Mutual
C = Spouse dominant
D = Self dominant

Question 39a—Qualities of good relationships:
A, C, D, E, H, I, J, K, L, M, N, O, P, Q, R = Intimate (count number)
B, F, G = Non-intimate (count number)

In general, any features related to closeness and intrinsic features of the relationship counts as intimate; practical features count as non-intimate.

Appendix D
Results

Demographic Characteristics of Sample

The sample's demographic characteristics are listed in Table 1. Overall demographic characteristics are displayed first followed by a listing of relevant variables according to the division of the sample by years married.

TABLE 1. Demographic characteristics.

Group	Mean	s.d.	Range
Total Sample			
Wife's occupation	7.22	1.34	2–9
Wife's education	16.70	2.28	12–20
Wife's SES	54.97	8.86	22–66
Husband's occupation	7.00	1.89	2–9
Husband's education	16.90	2.59	12–20
Husband's SES	53.18	11.20	30–66
Couple's SES	53.35	9.99	30–66
Married Ten Year or Less			
Wife's age	31.76	4.18	26–42
Husband's age	33.43	5.72	27–52
Years married	7.24	1.92	5–10
Number of children	.76	.89	0–3
Married Longer than Ten Years			
Wife's age	36.95	3.26	32–44
Husband's age	38.95	3.55	34–50
Years married	14.95	2.97	11–20
Number of children	2.05	1.17	0–5

Scores on Intimacy, Communication, and Dyadic Adjustment Scales

The means and standard deviations on the main variables of the study divided by groups on the basis of years married are shown in Table 2.

TABLE 2. Summary statistics for main variables of study.

Group	Mean	s.d.	Range
Married Ten Years or Less			
Accurate perception	29.65	5.13	21.45– 41.30
Perceived similarity	14.29	5.13	4.00– 23.00
Self-intimacy	18.83	2.59	13.50– 23.00
Communication	30.86	13.01	.00– 60.00
Egalitarianism	.90	.34	.35– 1.60
Wives' dyadic adjustment	114.19	12.13	91.00–133.0
Husbands' dyadic adjustment	113.76	14.92	80.00–139.0
Married Longer than Ten Years			
Accurate perception	29.92	3.88	23.67– 37.83
Perceived similarity	15.53	4.29	7.00– 23.00
Self-intimacy	18.26	3.66	11.00– 24.00
Communication	28.00	14.04	3.00– 52.00
Egalitarianism	.88	.29	.30– 1.25
Wives' dyadic adjustment	114.32	11.24	82.00–131.0
Husbands' dyadic adjustment	114.90	12.13	81.00–129.0

Prediction of Dyadic Adjustment Scores

Scores from the intimacy interview, communication task, and egalitarianism scale were entered in prediction equations with marital adjustment scores of husbands and wives as the dependent measures. Separate regression equations were estimated for the shorter- and longer-married couple groups.

The variables in each regression analyses were: Accurate perception scores, Perceived similarity scores, Self-intimacy scores, Egalitarianism scores, and the percent of "work" communication style rated for the couple's joint problem-solving task. The results of the regression analyses are shown in Table 3.

TABLE 3. Results of regression analyses for dyadic adjustment scores.

Variable in Equation	Change in R^2	F	p	Beta weight
Wives Married Ten Years or Less:				
Perceived similarity	.50	19.01	.001	1.67
Husbands Married Ten Years or Less:				
Self-intimacy	.45	15.36	.001	3.86
Wives Married Longer than Ten Years:				
Perceived similarity	.33	12.82	.002	1.75
Accurate perception	.15	4.56	.02	1.15
Husbands Married Longer than Ten Years:				
Perceived similarity	.25	5.61	.03	1.41

Intimacy Potential of Husbands and Its Relation to Marital Adjustment and Intimacy of Wives

An analysis reported in Chapter 2 concerned the interactive effects that spouses have on each other. The question investigated in this analysis was whether husbands with high intimacy potential could "improve" the intimacy potential of their wives. For this analysis, four groups were formed based on the combination of the self-intimacy and marital adjustment scores of husbands. These four groups represented the combination of high (above the median) and low (below the median) scorers on the self-intimacy and marital adjustment variables. The differences among the four groups was significant, both for self-intimacy, $F(3, 36) = 3.16$, $p < .04$, and marital adjustment, $F(3, 36) = 6.11$, $p < .002$. The means and standard deviations of the self-intimacy and marital adjustment scores of wives are shown in Table 4.

TABLE 4. Marital adjustment and intimacy of wives according to intimacy potential of husbands.

Variable and Group (based on husbands' scores)	Mean	s.d.	Range
Marital Adjustment of Wife:			
High marital adjustment/high self-intimacy	120.33	10.09	99–133
Low marital adjustment/high self-intimacy	118.44	9.29	104–129
High marital adjustment/low self-intimacy	114.50	7.46	100–123
Low marital adjustment/low self-intimacy	104.00	11.21	82–121
Self-intimacy of Wife:			
High marital adjustment/high self-intimacy	20.92	2.54	15–24
Low marital adjustment/high self-intimacy	19.89	3.66	15–25
High marital adjustment/low self-intimacy	17.88	3.52	12–22
Low marital adjustment/low self-intimacy	17.55	2.30	15–21

As can be seen from this table, the marital adjustment and self-intimacy scores of wives varied according to the intimacy potential of their husbands. Wives with high intimacy potential husbands were better adjusted and themselves had higher intimacy potential.

A similar analysis for husbands (based on the self-intimacy and marital adjustment scores of wives) revealed that the marital adjustment scores of husbands varied according to the marital adjustment scores of the wives, $F(3, 36) = 7.63$, $p < .0001$. The differences among the groups of husbands varied according to the marital adjustment of husbands, not their self-intimacy, as can be seen from Table 5. For husbands, in contrast to wives, having a spouse with low intimacy potential did not affect their own intimacy potential or marital adjustment. Instead, the marital adjustment of husbands varied directly as a function of the marital adjustment of their wives. Thus, the intimacy potential of wives did not have the effect of "pulling up" or "pulling down" the intimacy potential or adjustment of their husbands.

TABLE 5. Marital adjustment and intimacy of wives according to intimacy potential of husbands.

Variable and Group (based on wives' scores)	Mean	s.d.	Range
	Marital Adjustment of Husband:		
High marital adjustment/high self-intimacy	123.78	8.89	115–139
Low marital adjustment/high self-intimacy	112.20	8.43	95–120
High marital adjustment/low self-intimacy	119.91	10.22	103–139
Low marital adjustment/low self-intimacy	101.70	14.94	80–125

Satisfaction with the Sexual Relationship and Marital Adjustment in Husbands

Couples were grouped according to whether or not both spouses said that both they and their partners were satisfied with the sex in their relationship. The responses on which this grouping was based were to Questions 30a and 30b of the intimacy interview. The marital adjustment of husbands was found to differ significantly between these two groups for the longer-married sample only, $t(17) = 2.11$, $p < .05$. The means on which these analyses were based are shown in Table 6.

TABLE 6. Marital adjustment of husbands according to mutual sexual satisfaction of couple.

Group	Mean	s.d.	N
Couples Married Ten Years or Less:			
Both partners satisfied	118.90	14.78	10
Both partners not satisfied	109.09	14.07	11
Couples Married Longer than Ten Years:			
Both partners satisfied	120.56	5.27	9
Both partners not satisfied	109.80	14.44	10

As can be seen from this table, not only were the scores substantially higher in the older-married group with both partners satisfied (and believing their partners to be), but there was a narrower spread of scores than in the other groups. Given that this variable was the only one that uniquely identified the more well-adjusted husbands in the older-married group, it seems to be capturing an important aspect of the factors contributing to adjustment in this group.

Perceptions of Control Within the Relationship

Seven questions on the intimacy interview that made up the accuracy of perception score examined the perceptions of spouses concerning which partner had more influence. Four of these questions were about the practical aspects of relationship and three were about sexuality. The distribution of responses to these questions is shown in Table 7. Across both areas, wives were twice as likely as husbands to be seen as having more control (86 cases of wives versus 42 cases of husbands). Wives were more likely to have power attributed to them in the area of practical affairs, though, and husbands to be seen as having more control in the sexual domain.

TABLE 7. Perceptions of control by area of intimacy interview.

	Practical	Sexuality
Wife regarded as more in control	68	18
Husband regarded as more in control	8	34
(Chi square = 39.70, $p < .000001$)		

Table 7 shows a fuller breakdown within the practical domain of the distribution of responses by husbands and wives to the questions on the interview concerning power distribution.

TABLE 8. Perceptions of control within the practical domain.

	Plans	Major Decisions	Minor Decisions	Wishes take Precedence
Husband and wife agree:				
Wife is in control	5	1	15	3
Husband is in control	2	1	0	0
Husband says equal and wife says she is in control	8	5	5	12
Husband says wife is in control and wife says equal	4	3	5	2

Other possible combinations (wife says equal and husband says he is in control; husband says equal and wife says husband, etc.) contained mostly zeros.

As can be seen from this table, when power was unequivocally attributed to the wife in the practical domain, it was in the area of minor, everyday decision-making. Of the 40 couples, there was agreement among 15 (38%) by both partners that the wife played the major role. The situation differed considerably when husbands and wives disagreed about who was in control in the larger sense of whose wishes take precedence. As can be seen from Table 8, disagreements about who is the dominant partner in this aspect of the relationship are more likely to involve a difference in perception of whether the wife is in control or not. The husband's control is not at issue.

The Role of Communication

Couples were grouped according to whether both of them mentioned communication as important in answer to Question 39 of the intimacy interview. Subdivided by length of marriage, the communication scores are shown in Table 9.

TABLE 9. Communication scores according to reference to communication as important.

Group	Mean	s.d.	N
Couples Married Ten Years or Less:			
Important to both partners	37.20	9.96	10
Not important to both	25.09	13.13	11
Couples Married Longer than Ten Years:			
Important to both partners	30.38	13.30	8
Not important to both	26.27	14.93	11

The difference between the groups was significant for the shorter-married only, $t(17) = 2.36$, $p < .03$. This finding can be interpreted as indicating that for these couples, both saying communication is important differentiates them in their actual behavior; the same does not hold true for the longer-married couples.

References

Beckman, L. & Houser, B. (1979). The more you have, the more you do: The relationship between wife's employment, sex-role attitudes, and household behavior. *Psychology of Women Quarterly*, *4*, 160–174.

Bernard, J. (1973). *The future of marriage*. New York: Bantam Books.

Ebmeyer, J. (1982). *And baby makes three: A comparative study of dual-worker couples with and without a child*. Unpublished manuscript, University of Rochester.

Erikson, E. (1963). *Childhood and society* (2nd Ed.). New York: W.W. Norton.

Gould, R. (1978). *Transformations: Growth and change in adult life*. New York: Simon & Shuster.

Hollingshead, A.B. (1979). *A four-factor index of social status*. Unpublished manuscript, Yale University.

Levinger, G. (1977). Re-viewing the close relationship. In G. Levinger & H. Raush (Eds.), *Close relationships: Perspectives on the meaning of intimacy*. Amherst: University of Massachusetts Press.

Miller, S., Nunnally, E., & Wackman, D. (1975). *Alive and aware: Improving communication in relationships*. Minneapolis, MN: Interpersonal Communication Programs.

Orlofsky, J., Marcia, J., & Lesser, I. (1973). Ego identity status and the intimacy versus isolation crisis of young adulthood. *Journal of Personality and Social Psychology*, *27*, 211–219.

Perucci, C., Potter, H., & Rhoads, D. (1978). Determinants of male family role performance. *Psychology of Women Quarterly*, *3*, 53–66.

Rubin, L. (1983). *Intimate strangers*. New York: Harper & Row.

Schaefer, M. & Olson, D. (1981). Assessing intimacy: The PAIR inventory. *Journal of Marriage and Family Therapy*, *7*, 47–60.

Spanier, G.B. (1976). Measuring dyadic adjustment: New scales for assessing the quality of marriage and similar dyads. *Journal of Marriage and the Family*, *38*, 15–28.

Tesch, S. & Whitbourne, S.K. (1982). Intimacy and identity status in young adults. *Journal of Personality and Social Psychology*, *43*, 1041–1051.

Wampler, K. (1979). The effect of ego development on the learning and retention of communication skills. *Dissertation Abstracts International*, *40* b, 2860B, University Microfilms No. 7926442.

Whitbourne, S.K. (1986a). *Adult development* (2nd Ed.). New York: Praeger.

Whitbourne, S.K. (1986b). *The me I know: A study of adult identity*. New York: Springer-Verlag.

Index